THE TREASURE OF THE GREAT REEF

THE
TREASURE
OF THE
GREAT REEF

by Arthur C. Clarke
with Mike Wilson

HARPER & ROW, PUBLISHERS

NEW YORK AND EVANSTON

To
Artie, Vida and
the Wayne Family Robinson

Contents

Illustrations

The following illustrations will be found after page 142:

Acknowledgments

Among the many people and institutions who assisted us in this project, we would especially like to thank:

Peter Throckmorton, who abandoned his own work at a moment's notice to join us.

Frank Rees, O.B.E., and his successor, Lieutenant Commander E. W. de la Mare, R.N.R., of the Imperial Lighthouse Service, for the hospitality of the Great Basses Lighthouse.

The Avon Rubber Company for their gift of two REDSHANK dinghies, without which operations on the Reef would have been impossible.

Colin McLeod, of Messrs. Lillywhites, London, for assistance with equipment.

Montres Rolex, Geneva, for underwater watches.

Mendel Peterson, of the Smithsonian Institution, for his technical advice.

The Imperial Lighthouse staff at Kirinda, for good-naturedly sharing their accommodation with us.

Major R. Raven-Hart, and the ladies of Writer's & Speaker's Research, London, for much digging into dusty archives.

Dr. C. E. Godakumbure, and the staff of the Department of Archaeology, Colombo, for cooperating with us in the investigation and protection of this unique site.

THE TREASURE OF THE GREAT REEF

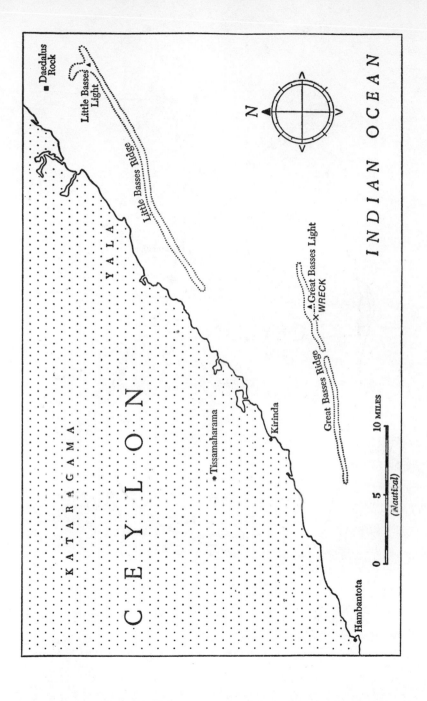

■ Daedalus
Rock

Little Basses ▲
Light

Little Basses Ridge

▲ Great Basses Light
× ··· WRECK

Great Basses Ridge

• Tissamaharama

Kirinda •

KATARAGAMA

C E Y L O N

Y A L A

Hambantota •

INDIAN OCEAN

N

0   5   10 MILES
(Nautical)

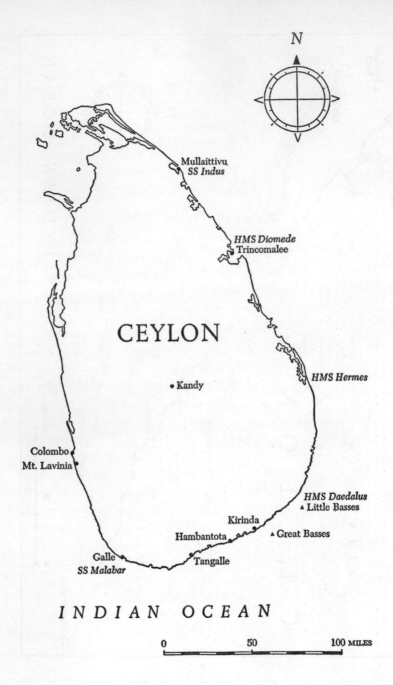

N

Mullaittivu
SS *Indus*

HMS *Diomede*
Trincomalee

CEYLON

• Kandy

HMS *Hermes*

Colombo •
Mt. Lavinia •

HMS *Daedalus*
▲ Little Basses

Kirinda
Hambantota ▲ Great Basses

Galle •
SS *Malabar*   Tangalle

INDIAN OCEAN

0   50   100 MILES

1

Of Time

and Treasure

Nothing, except perhaps the landing of a fly-
ing saucer in one's backyard, is quite so disruptive of everyday
life as the discovery of sunken treasure. There are very few
people in the world who can confirm this, but by a series of
most unlikely events I happen to be among them. This book
is the story of that experience, which I would not have missed
for anything—but under no circumstances would wish to re-
peat; for it cost me my health and very nearly my life.

When one considers the amount of treasure that the sea has
swallowed, it appears surprising that so little has been recovered. Every few years, we read in the papers of an expedition (complete with "authentic" map) setting off hopefully
after the loot of Captain Kidd or Sir Henry Morgan; we never
hear of its successful return. Why not?

Let us look at the statistics. According to John Potter's *The
Treasure Diver's Guide* (Doubleday, 1960), the figures for
the most important of the historic treasure routes are roughly
as follows:

1. Spanish armadas—Caribbean to Spain (1500-1820) $8
billion carried, $400 million lost.

2. Peru transports—Peru to Spain *via* Cape Horn (1534-1810) $2 billion carried, $50 million lost.

3. Manila Galleons—Acapulco to Philippines (1570-1815) $1 billion carried, $50 million lost.

4. The Spice Route—Europe and the Far East (1502-1870) $2 billion carried, $50 million lost.

Even though these figures can only be the roughest approximations, the general picture is clear. During the last four centuries, several hundred millions in gold and silver have been paid as homage to the sea. Most of it is still there.

Most, but certainly not all. Whenever a valuable cargo goes down in a known and accessible spot, it is always promptly salvaged. Because it has made such great strides during the last fifty years, we tend to think of diving as a modern accomplishment—but, of course, it is not. For thousands of years there have been men who could do active work at depths of a hundred feet or more, and as most ships are lost on reefs or in shallow water, naked divers were often able to do a surprisingly good job of salvage. For this reason, any treasure ship that went down in a known area is probably no longer of interest. It is surprising how few people realize this apparently obvious fact; if a treasure map is indeed authentic—the treasure has already gone.

But this still leaves quite a few hundred millions at the bottom of the sea. Some of this lies in water too deep for salvage work, even when its location is accurately known—which is never the case. The *Thresher* tragedy showed how difficult it is, with virtually unlimited resources, to find a vessel that has recently gone down in a fairly well-defined area. How hopeless, then, would be the task of looking for a centuries-old galleon that had sunk "somewhere" in the Atlantic or Pacific!

The really interesting and worthwhile treasure wrecks are those that ran aground on unmarked, lonely reefs. In such a case, the crew may escape in the boats, but even when this happens, the exact site of the disaster may never be known.

More often there will be no survivors at all, and the ship will vanish from the sight of man—as so many thousands have done and still do even to this day.

Picture one of these abandoned hulks, just after it has run aground, lying awash on some Pacific or Caribbean reef. It may be in excellent condition, much of its canvas still aloft, its hull scarcely damaged, the wealth it carries still safely stowed. But after a few seasons, the waves will smash it to pieces and scatter its cargo far and wide. For a year or so, the seabed may be carpeted with gold and silver—a fortune lying to be picked up by anyone who can hold his breath for thirty seconds. This must have happened many, many times along the great treasure routes of the past; and only the wandering seagulls knew.

The lost treasure will lie glittering in the open for only a very few years; soon, the heavy gold will work itself into the seabed, the silver will start to corrode. And all the while mud and sand will be sweeping over the wreck—or, if it is in the tropics, the busy corals will be building their homes over every square inch of exposed surface. Within fifty years, a diver might swim above the wreck—and notice nothing. Within a century, ship and treasure will lie beneath yards of mud, or sealed within a blanket of coral a foot thick, and hard as concrete.

Against such odds as this, the finding of a lost treasure wreck is almost a miracle. For years, divers have been combing the Caribbean; yet to my knowledge, only two (Arthur McKee and Teddy Tucker) have made worthwhile discoveries in modern times.

But miracles sometimes happen, especially to those who are prepared for them. In the spring of 1961, on the old Spice Route to India, one happened to us.

2

The Isle
of Taprobane

But first, as the persuasive gentlemen in the
TV commercials are fond of saying, a word about the background of this story and the characters involved. There are six
in the opening scenes, three of them human.

The lead is undoubtedly my energetic partner Mike Wilson.
I first met Mike around 1951, as a teenage (and, therefore,
illegal) intruder in the pub frequented by the London science-fiction fraternity. Every Thursday about fifty of us used
to meet to discuss the books and stories we had read, and
those we would write whenever we happened to have the
time. This background I later immortalized, if that is the correct word, in *Tales from the "White Hart."*

A smoke-filled saloon bar off wet and foggy Fleet Street
was a strange place to learn about skindiving on coral reefs.
Mike, who had done this during a spell in the British Merchant Navy, infected me with his enthusiasm, and I was soon
learning to use flippers and face mask in a London swimming
pool. After a few chilly dips in the English Channel (including an aqualung dive to eighty feet in midwinter), we de-

cided that this was a hobby for the tropics. I traveled west to Florida, Mike east to Australia, where we eventually rendezvoused on the Great Barrier Reef—the 1,200 mile long belt of islands and shoals that runs up the Queensland coast from the Tropic of Capricorn almost to New Guinea.

I have described our first small expedition, which took place in 1955, in *The Coast of Coral*; it is significant here because both Mike and I passed through Ceylon on our way to Australia, and both decided independently that we would like to come back and spend more time in the island. We were able to do this in 1956, and the first result was *The Reefs of Taprobane*.

Taprobane (now rhymes with "rain" though a few classical scholars still accent the final "e") is the ancient Greek name for Ceylon; the island has had many names, some of them extremely beautiful. ("Serendip," origin of the overworked word serendipity, is one.) Most Europeans have heard of Ceylon and are vaguely aware that it is somewhere near India; few Americans, I regret to say, even know that it exists, and those who do are liable to misplace it. My erudite friend Willy Ley, in the preface to a recent edition of *Rockets, Missiles and Space Travel*, charged me with having "abandoned the Northern Hemisphere for Ceylon." I was under exactly the same misapprehension until I came here; actually, the most southerly part of the island—and the locale of the adventures in this book—is six degrees *north* of the equator.

When we arrived in Colombo in January 1956, neither Mike nor I had the faintest idea that we would still be here seven years later. I mention this as a warning to anyone else who thinks he is immune to the island's spell. A short visit—say one or two weeks—is probably harmless, and may even be an effective antitoxin if customs officials and weather are uncooperative; but anything over a couple of months may have serious consequences. Though I have never discovered any lotus blossoms in the famous Botanical Gardens at

Kandy, the mountain capital of Ceylon, I suspect that they are there.

It is true that we escaped occasionally on lecture tours of the United States, but we were never away for long and our absences grew shorter and shorter, until eventually a year at a time would pass without either of us leaving the island. There was plenty to do here; I was kept busy with my writing, while Mike tried, without much success, to build up a small diving business. As we had brought with us an air-compressor, aqualungs, and numerous underwater cameras, it seemed a pity not to use them; so Mike joined forces with Rodney Jonklaas, the diver-naturalist who assisted us on our earlier expedition, and issued a brochure announcing his willingness to tackle any underwater job.

Anyone who thinks that professional diving is a glamorous occupation should be disabused by what happened to Mike and Rodney. The mainstay of their business was cleaning the water inlet and sewage outlet grilles of ships in Colombo Harbor. These essential orifices get rapidly clogged, especially when a ship is anchored for some weeks in tropical waters, and divers can reach them much more easily using aqualungs than wearing the clumsy helmet and rubber suit. As Rodney put it, he and Mike were the highest paid lavatory coolies in Asia.

Even less attractive was the task, which arose all too often, of retrieving corpses in various stages of disrepair. One day there was an SOS from a large engineering firm, whose new reinforced concrete bridge had collapsed into the swollen, muddy waters of a local river—carrying a workman down into the depths. A hostile crowd of more than a thousand villagers had gathered, demanding that the body be found and properly buried before work on the bridge proceeded; so Mike, with a U.S. Marine Corps friend as back-up diver, descended into the tangle of twisted reinforcing bars and broken concrete. Fighting a strong current and working by touch in absolutely zero visibility (the water was virtually liquid mud), he managed to retrieve the victim. For thus risking his life, he charged sixty dollars—all of which he gave to the unfortunate man's widow. There was, clearly, no future in this sort of thing.

The most ambitious and spectacular job that Mike and Rodney tackled during their professional partnership was at Castlereagh Dam, a great hydroelectric project four thousand feet up in the central mountains of Ceylon. This involved going eighty feet down into the cold, dead waters of an artificial lake, making a vertical U-turn, and then climbing up a slot only eighteen inches wide. The massive steel doors which closed the tunnel leading to the turbines, a quarter of a mile further down the mountain, were supposed to move up and down in this slot, but they were blocked by protruding metal bars which Mike and Rodney had to cut away.

A helmet diver, in his bulky suit, could not possibly have reached the site; nor could an aqualung diver carrying a tank on his back. The only solution was, in effect, to split the aqualung into two parts, keeping the tanks on the surface and connecting them to the diver by a pipeline. After four weeks of hard and dangerous work with this "hookah" system, Mike and Rodney had cleared the slots and earned enough to buy a Volkswagen van; but they had also decided that there must be much easier ways of making a living.

Rodney found his answer in the fish business; I don't mean fish to eat, but fish to watch. The reefs around Ceylon are crowded with beautiful marine butterflies in an unbelievable variety of forms and colors; Rodney knows exactly where to look for any given specimen, and equally important, the right technique for catching it. His knowledge of the waters round the island is quite uncanny; let me give an example from personal experience.

One day the three of us were taking an experimental fiberglass boat (a design of Mike's, with which he hoped to revolutionize the local fishing industry) up a deserted stretch of the east coast, miles and miles from anywhere. The sea became rather rough, so we decided to put into a small creek—a narrow river mouth surrounded by jungle. It was easy to believe that we were the first human beings ever to visit this isolated spot. Presently, as we nibbled sandwiches on the shore, Rodney pointed to a group of rocks a few yards out to sea and remarked casually, "There's a family of scorpion fish living under those. I think I'll try to catch them." And he did.

Exporting tropical fish is a highly specialized and scientific business, made possible only by air transportation and polythene, in that order. Air freight allows the living cargo to be rushed from supplier to customer within forty-eight hours, and polythene bags provide the necessary lightweight, unbreakable, waterproof containers. Sealed in these bags, the airspace above them pumped full of oxygen, fish can survive for days. The greatest risk that Rodney's stock-in-trade has to run is being off-loaded for a few freezing hours in midwinter at Idlewild or London Airport, but nowadays such disasters are rare.

While Rodney built up his export business (almost every large aquarium now has some of his colorful captives in its tanks), Mike tried his hand at a variety of occupations. I have already mentioned the fiberglass boat project, which eventually sank without trace after about six months' work. Then he launched "Submarine Safaris," proposing to show tourists the underwater beauties of Ceylon. Leaflets and posters were printed, and brought in exactly one client. Perhaps it was just as well; Mike is not the sort of person who suffers fools gladly, and if he had had to cope with underwater tourists, it would have been only a matter of time before he failed to bring one back.

We had chosen, I suppose, the worst possible time to settle down in Ceylon. In 1956 the Western-orientated, conservative government of Sir John Kotelawala (which had lost contact with the people, as all conservative governments eventually do) was annihilated at the polls, and replaced by an unstable left-wing coalition headed by Mr. S. W. R. D. Bandaranaike. "Banda," as everyone called him (the name is not difficult to pronounce, if you say "Ban-dar-an-aye-ah-ka" without pausing for breath), was typical of the Oxford, London-School-of-Economics intellectuals who have played so important a role in transforming the British Empire into the British Commonwealth—not always to the comfort of the British. A sincere and brilliant man, with his country's interests genuinely at heart, he was unable to cope with the extremists surrounding him and the situation deteriorated until, in 1958, it erupted into a state of emergency. In places, this was not far from a small-scale civil war between the two main racial groups, the Sinhalese (about 70 per cent of the population) and the Tamils (about 20 per cent).

The full story of the 1958 emergency has never been published and probably never will be. It is generally believed that there were about a thousand deaths, and much property damage was done; but perhaps worse was the harm caused to Sinhalese-Tamil relations. Ceylon was divided into two nations, neither trusting the other, with fanatical extremists working on both sides to prevent the *rapprochement* the country so desperately needed.

The emergency caused us no trouble; at its height, the only inconvenience was the 6 P.M. curfew. Even this did not worry Mike, who promptly placed his Landrover and himself at the disposal of the police and so got a pass to go out whenever he wished. As far as I know, only one European was killed during the emergency, and that was largely his own fault. He was out during curfew while drunk, and failed to halt when challenged.

The disturbances swiftly died away, and the country went once more about its business. But next year there was a potentially worse crisis, when—for reasons which are still politically obscure—a Buddhist monk assassinated the prime minister.

This outrage shocked the country into a kind of remorseful calm; I have never seen such queues—they were literally miles long—as those that filed past the prime minister's coffin as he lay in state. A caretaker government took over, was defeated at the polls, and quietly made way for its successor. After several elections, conducted for the most part with a rectitude that would do credit to any democracy, Mr. Bandaranaike's widow scored a remarkable personal triumph and became the world's first woman prime minister. There have been no further disturbances, and though it faces many problems (most of them basically economic, for the island depends on the three crops of tea, rubber, and coconut products to pay for its imports), Ceylon is probably the most stable country in the Far East, next to India and Japan.

Today there are many shortages, many handicaps, many inconveniences (not least one of the highest rates of taxation in the world), affecting anyone who resides in Ceylon. Yet somehow, such is the charm and beauty of the country and the friendliness of its people, these things scarcely matter. Though I never left England until I was thirty-three years old (or traveled more than a score of miles from my birthplace until I was twenty), it is Ceylon, not England, that now seems home.

I do not pretend to account for this, or for the fact that no other place is now wholly real to me. Though London, Washington, New York, Los Angeles, are exciting, amusing, invigorating, and hold all the things that interest my mind, they are no longer quite convincing. Their images are blurred around the edges; like a mirage, they will not stand up to detailed inspection. When I am in the Strand, or 42nd Street, or NASA Headquarters, or the Beverly Hills Hotel (and recently I visited them all within a few weeks), my surroundings are liable to give a sudden tremor, and I see through the insubstantial fabric to the reality beneath.

And always it is the same; the slender palm trees leaning over the white sand, the warm sun sparkling on the waves as they break on the inshore reef, the outrigger fishing boats drawn up high on the beach. This alone is real; the rest is but a dream from which I shall presently awake.

3

The Great Reef

Though Ceylon is the background against which our adventure took place, its actual locale is a spot which few Ceylonese have seen and fewer still have visited. It is a wave-swept line of submerged rocks, running parallel to the south coast of the island at a distance of about six miles, and bearing the curious name "Great Basses." This, we later discovered, comes from the Portuguese *Baxios*, ("a reef or shoal"); so "Great Basses" simply means "Great Reef."

A glance at the map shows that the Great Basses—and its sister reef the Little Basses, a few miles to the east—might have been specially designed to snare ships rounding the southern coast of Ceylon. This double trap lies directly across one of the main trade routes of the Oriental world; every ship of any size passing the longitude of India has to contend with it. (The narrow passage to the north of Ceylon, full of shifting sandbanks and almost blocked by the submerged land ridge known as Adam's Bridge, is not navigable except by very small craft at certain seasons.) For at least three thousand years the twin reefs must have taken their toll of shipping; it is conceivable that there has been a greater concentration of wrecks here than anywhere in the world outside the Mediterranean or the Aegean.

Even in daylight, during perfectly calm weather, ships have

12

come to grief on the Basses; later in this book I shall give an
eyewitness account of one such disaster. And at night, the
two reefs must have presented an appalling hazard to ships,
especially when they were being driven landwards by the
winds of the southwest monsoon.

Not until the middle of the nineteenth century could anything be done about this danger. By then, however, progress
in engineering had made it practical to construct lighthouses
on such remote, wave-swept rocks, and the government of
Ceylon, alarmed by the continual losses in this area, gave orders for work to proceed.

The first attempt to erect a lighthouse on the Great Basses
was a total failure; after the British Board of Trade had sunk
£40,000 into the project (say $250,000 of today's currency),
all it had to show for its money and three years of work was
a solitary flag pole on the rock. Though a lighthouse made of
cast-iron had been built in England and shipped out to Ceylon, no one could manage to get it across the remaining ten
miles of sea to the reef.

A new approach was obviously needed, and it was provided by Trinity House,[1] the London corporation responsible for matters affecting the safety of shipping. The
cast-iron lighthouse was shipped off in disgrace to the Baha-
mas (where, as far as I know, it may still be doing a good job),
and an all-granite version was designed in 1867 by Sir J. N.
Douglass, the engineer of Trinity House and builder of the
famous Eddystone Light. For advice on the construction of
the lantern itself, one of the greatest scientists of the nineteenth century was called in—Michael Faraday, whose discoveries made possible the age of electricity.

The thousands of tons of granite were carved and assembled in Scotland; then the blocks were carefully numbered

---

[1] Or, to give its full title "The Guild, Fraternity or Brotherhood of the
Most Glorious and Undivided Trinity and of St. Clement in the parish of
Depford Stronde in the County of Kent." Modern corporation lawyers,
please copy.

and shipped to Ceylon. Only one of the more than a thousand blocks was damaged in its transit halfway round the world, and even that caused no delay, for the engineers had thoughtfully provided spares.

The actual job of erection on the reef was supervised by William Douglass, brother of the designer, and having seen what he was up against, I have an enormous respect for him. The huge blocks of granite (two or three tons in weight) were carried out to the site from the port of Galle, sixty miles to the west, in two small steamers specially built for the job. In the first year, a crane was set up on the reef, and with its aid the blocks were slung ashore. In the second year, most of the tower was built, and in the third, it was completed. The ruby beams began their circling on March 10, 1873, and have flashed every night from sunset to sunrise ever since.

There can be few men who have left a better monument than the Douglass brothers; think of them, if you ever round Ceylon on a stormy night.

Mike and Rodney made their first visit to the Great Basses Reef in 1958, taking out all their equipment from the mainland each day in the small fiberglass dinghy we had christened *J. Y. Cousteau*, after our patron saint. This twenty-mile trip across dangerous waters in a light, open boat loaded with diving gear was a hair-raising (not to mention harebrained) performance which I am very glad to have missed. When we went out again the following year, matters were much better organized; thanks to the courtesy of the Imperial Lighthouse Service, we lived in the lighthouse and used that as our base.

Since I have devoted a book (*Indian Ocean Adventure*) to this expedition, I will mention only the highlights of the week we spent exploring the world of the Great Basses Reef. We had chosen our time—April—with care, for it is only possible to dive on Great Basses for a short period every year. For almost ten months out of the twelve, the weather is so rough that it is difficult even to approach the lighthouse, and quite impossible to land. The rock on which the tower is built is not much larger than a tennis court, and is nowhere more than three feet above the waterline. Even in calm weather, waves are liable to break over it at any moment.

Fortunately, the good season can be predicted with a fair degree of accuracy. This is because the Indian Ocean has a mysteriously regular system of winds—the famous monsoons —which come and go almost according to the calendar. Between October and March the wind blows from the northeast; then it slackens, and there are about two months of calm weather. But between April and May the wind switches to the other direction; the southwest monsoon sets in, with heavy rain and violent storms. The only time that operations on the reef are possible, therefore, is through March and April; and we could not always count on this, for the monsoon is not absolutely reliable. But in 1959 we were lucky; we had almost perfect weather.

Both the Great and Little Basses lighthouses are serviced by a relief boat based at a little fishing village with the lovely name of Kirinda. (Somewhat easier than many Ceylon place names: my favorites include Angunakolapelessa, Illuppadichhandiya—one could quote these lockjaw recipes for several pages.) At Kirinda, the Imperial Lighthouse Service maintains a stoutly built powerboat, the *Pharos,* with a crew of skilled seamen who know how to get her out to the reef, unload a couple of tons of stores, and bring her safely back.

Because the *Pharos* sailed before dawn, when the sea was at its calmest, we had to be on Kirinda Beach at the hideous hour of 4 A.M., and our aqualungs, underwater cameras, compressed-air tanks, drums of gas, canned food, weight belts, air compressor, and other gear were loaded in the dark, being carried out on the heads of husky Kirindans wading through the surf. It was a clear, starry night, and above us the constellations of the equator hung at angles I had never seen before, being too addicted to sleep to be a good astronomer.

Out on the horizon, ten miles away, the bright ruby flash of the lighthouse flickered every forty-five seconds. As we drew away from land, I could not help wondering when we would get back to civilization. The relief boat was due to pick us up again in five days, but there had been times when it was delayed for weeks by bad weather. If this happened, we would certainly not starve; but we might get rather tired of eating fish.

We were several miles out to sea when dawn broke, not as quickly as it usually does in the tropics, but almost slowly through low banks of clouds. A few minutes before the sun finally appeared, its beams fanned out across the sky in great luminous spokes, like those of a slowly turning wheel. It was a spectacle I had seen on such a scale only once before, when I was sailing back to the mainland of Australia from the Great Barrier Reef. Then it had been a symbol of farewell, but now it heralded a new adventure. And I thought how perfectly Homer had described the sight three thousand years ago, when he wrote of the "rosy-fingered dawn."

An hour later, the coast of Ceylon was only a low, misty band far behind, dimpled bluely here and there by the inland mountains. It no longer seemed to have any connection with us; all that mattered now was the white column of stone rearing starkly from the waters ahead. Around the base of the lighthouse the waves were breaking continuously at the end of their long march from Antarctica, the nearest land to the south. Every few seconds the exposed reef would be completely hidden by foam, so that only the lower platform of the lighthouse was visible. It was difficult to imagine how we could land—or, having landed, get off again.

For the next ten minutes we watched with anxious interest while the crew maneuvered to get us and our equipment onto those wetly gleaming rocks. The *Pharos* had been towing a large surfboat, in which we traveled with our stores, and while she stood by at a respectful distance this was rowed through the bucking waves until it came to within fifty feet of the reef. Then two anchors were let out, spaced well apart to keep the boat from being dragged onto the rocks.

The men on the lighthouse had been waiting, and as soon as our boat had come close enough they threw us a rope. The other end of this passed over the pulley of a sturdy crane bolted to the stone platform at the foot of the lighthouse.

Now the surfboat was secured at three points; by pulling on one or more of the ropes, the crew could hold it at a fixed distance from the reef. There was nothing they could do, however, to prevent it from rising and falling in the swell. At one moment we would be several feet above the level of the lighthouse platform; a second later, in the trough of a wave, we would be several feet below.

So that we could travel along the aerial ropeway now linking us to the rock, wooden bars had been lashed beneath it to act as seats. Perched on these, we were hauled up to the lighthouse, swinging back and forth with our feet just above the waves. And up that same rope, during the next two hours, went all our equipment, carefully packed in watertight containers.

Then followed the hardest work I have ever done (or ever will do) in my life. Merely living in the lighthouse was a strange and often exhausting experience. The temperature was always in the nineties, and we had to keep climbing up and down a spiral stairway a hundred feet high as we moved from one room to another. After a while I began to develop a fellow feeling for such creatures as snails and the chambered nautilus. Everything was curved; it was impossible to walk more than a few paces in a straight line, and I had to learn to sleep in the arc of a circle, for the bunks were neatly tucked into the yard thick walls.

We had arrived at the lighthouse in midmorning, and as soon as we had unpacked our equipment and had a meal, we prepared to dive. And this involved problems, for the Great Basses is certainly no place for beginners. Indeed, we had been told that it was utterly impossible to swim around the reef, and at first sight this seemed to be perfectly true.

For though the sea was now quite calm, the water was never still for a second; the level could rise or fall a couple of yards almost instantly over the jagged, barnacled rocks. Getting in and out of the water—especially when wearing an aqualung and carrying one or often two heavy cameras—therefore required good timing and strong nerves. You had to wait for the crest of a wave, and then literally throw yourself and your gear into the sea. If you missed, you were liable to be cut to ribbons on the barnacles.

It was impossible to do any exploring really close to the reef, because the surge of the water made it far too dangerous and also stirred up such clouds of bubbles that visibility was reduced to zero. We had to aim for deeper, calmer water a couple of hundred feet away, and getting there involved fighting strong currents which always seemed to be against us, whether we were coming or going. To serve as a mobile base while we were working over the reef, we had brought along an inflatable rubber dinghy which we could anchor wherever we pleased. Our circular raft was scarcely well streamlined, and to make matters worse, the aqualung cylinders dangling beneath it caused additional drag. It usually took about twenty minutes of steady flippering to reach the spot we had aimed at, less than a hundred yards from the lighthouse.

But the struggle was worth it. Beneath us was a fantastic fairyland of caves, grottoes, coral-encrusted valleys—and fish in such numbers as I have never met anywhere else in the world. Sometimes they crowded round us so closely that we could see nothing but a solid wall of scales, and had literally to push our way through it. They were inquisitive and completely unafraid; during our visit we met, in addition to the usual menagerie of small multicolored reef dwellers, eagle-rays, turtles, angelfish, jacks, tuna (up to 300 pounds!), groupers, and sharks. Especially the latter.

One of our chief objects in coming to the reef was to get some good shark pictures; though we had encountered sharks scores of times in the past, we had never taken any really good photographs of them—they were always too shy. We had hoped that the oceangoing sharks out here on the reef would be a little less nervous than the inshore ones; this proved to be the case, and we were able to get near them without difficulty.

Sharks locate their food in at least three ways, and possibly in others not yet discovered. They can see it, smell it, and hear it; in our experiments, we attracted them by appealing to all three senses.

Rodney would spear a fish, and as it struggled on the end of his harpoon, a shark would almost always appear within seconds. It could not have scented the blood—which takes a long time to disperse through water—so it must have been attracted by some sound or vibration.

The sea is full of noises, though we can seldom hear them because our ears have evolved to work in air, not in water. When a fish is injured, it struggles and the frantic fluttering of its fins make some distinctive noise which the other fish can recognize—and which they treat either as a warning or a dinner gong.

Waiting for the first shark to appear, when Rodney had shot his bait, was always an exciting experience. There would be the three of us on the seabed—Mike and I with cameras, Rodney reeling in the fish on his wire harpoon line—keeping a lookout to all quarters of the compass. Suddenly one of us would point, hooting into his aqualung mouthpiece at the same time to attract attention. At the edge of vision, a gray ghost slipping through the underwater haze, would be a perfectly streamlined torpedo, orbiting round us in a great circle at a distance of eighty or a hundred feet.

What happened next depended on the shark; if it was nervous, or well fed, it would disappear again within a few seconds. But if hunger overcame caution, then it would come spiraling in toward us, apparently without the slightest effort. For all its potential menace, a shark on the prowl is one of the most beautiful sights in the animal kingdom as it glides silently through the sea. Its tail and fins scarcely seem to do anything, except when it changes direction in a hurry. Then there will be a sudden flick of its tail—and it will stop dead in its tracks, or shoot off on a new course at incredible speed.

Although it was easy enough to get photographs of sharks, it was considerably more difficult to get men and sharks in the same picture. To do this, we tried an experiment which I do not recommend as a model, but which was not really as dangerous as it sounds.

Rodney shot a fish and tethered it to the seabed, gutting it so that there was plenty of blood in the water. I took up a position about ten feet away from the bait—*up*stream of the blood, needless to say—and lay flat on the seabed. Mike placed himself twenty feet to one side, so that he could get both me and the bait (we hoped that the two would not be synonymous) in the same field of view.

In cold print, this behavior may appear extremely reckless —even foolhardy; I certainly would not recommend it in Australian waters, where sharks kill several swimmers every year. The Ceylon sharks, however, have a clean record; there has never been a case of a man being killed—or even injured—by one. We suspect that this is because they are too well fed to bother about such an unusual item of diet.

Moreover, there were three of us, well armed with spears or heavy cameras. (A Rolleimarine case makes an excellent club at close quarters, though this is not very good for the camera.) We were in water so crystal clear that we could see a shark approaching from a hundred feet away, and would have plenty of warning if it showed signs of being aggressive. Speaking for myself, my chief worry was that the sight of three such strange creatures, blowing out streams of bubbles from their aqualungs, would scare the sharks away from the neighborhood.

I need not have worried. Almost at once a fairly large shark, about eight feet in length, appeared downcurrent. It began to swim back and forth in wide arcs, hunting over the seabed as it tried to locate the source of the blood. This "quartering" is characteristic of all animals, on land or sea, that use scent to locate their prey; a bloodhound weaves to and fro in wide sweeps until it has found the trail. Then it moves directly to its goal; and so did this shark.

It took no notice of me at all, as I lay flat on the seabed only ten feet away. Just as it was about to grab the fish, another and equally large shark came in like a thunderbolt. The battle was so swift that no human eye could have followed the details; all I can remember is a blur of gray and white bodies, twisting and turning in the water. As an example of sheer ferocity and power, I have never seen anything to match this silent collision on the seabed; two dogs fighting over a single bone give only a faint idea of its speed and violence. It was over in a second, lasting just long enough to be illuminated by the lightning stroke of Mike's flash bulb. Then the victor swept past me, gulping down the spoils, and leaving me to reflect that for the real meaning of the phrase "struggle for existence," one must look to the sea, not the land. Even the jungle is almost peaceful by comparison.

Our experiments with sharks ended somewhat abruptly, when Rodney harpooned a fish and was charged by a large and aggressive shark before he could get it off his spear. The fish was still struggling violently, and it was doubtless these vibrations that excited the shark. It swept round Rodney in great spirals, slowly closing in with each revolution. As his gun was now unloaded, Rodney was in a very uncomfortable position; he kept spinning round in the water to face the shark, holding his empty gun out in front of him like a pike.

Sometimes the shark would make a hairpin bend and double back on its tracks, and at least once it came close enough for Rodney to nudge it with his gun. It did not give up until Rodney had retreated to the dinghy, and had thrown the speared fish into it. No longer able to smell its hoped-for dinner, and deciding that Rodney was too large a mouthful, the disappointed shark made off into the distance. So determined an attack is quite unusual, but is another proof of the statement that one can never tell what a shark will do next.

Though the sharks were the most dramatic—and dangerous—of the reef's inhabitants, they were not the most interesting. I have not forgotten that, a couple of chapters ago, I mentioned that only three of the six characters involved in the opening of this story were human. Now it is time to meet the others.

4

The Cave

of Ali Baba

Wherever there are caves or wrecks in any of the world's tropical seas, there is one fish you are certain to meet. This is the Grouper—also known as the Sea Bass, Jewfish, or Sea Perch. The Grouper family has many members, some of them small and beautiful, others huge and ugly. The Australian pearl divers fear the really big ones much more than sharks; they have enormous mouths that open like trap doors, and they have been known to attack men. Often reaching a weight of over 1,000 pounds, they are completely fearless. With their massive, underslung jaws they look rather like bulldogs—and they can be equally stubborn and determined.

Groupers have had a hard time since underwater hunting became popular; in almost any issue of *Skin Diver* you will find a photograph of some intrepid sportsman standing beside a few hundred pounds of speared grouper. (The fish, though dead, usually looks the more intelligent of the two.) As a result they have been almost wiped out in the Mediterranean, where they were once common, and now one has to go to out-of-the-way places to find them. We were sure that we would meet them on the Great Basses Reef, and we were right.

On our very first dive, we discovered not just one grouper but a family of three (species *Epinephelus Fuscoguttatus*— the Black Grouper), with very different sizes and personalities. They came solemnly out of their caves to inspect us, but kept their distance until Rodney had speared a fish. Then hunger got the better of caution; the largest of the groupers darted at the struggling fish, and tried to wrench it off the spear. But as the barbs on the harpoon had now opened, it could not do so, and Rodney was quickly involved in an underwater tug-of-war. With considerable difficulty, as he was being jerked back and forth on the seabed, he managed to unscrew the barbed head of his spear, slip off the harpooned fish, and hand it to the surprised grouper—who now accepted it quite gently. This was the beginning of a touching though somewhat boisterous friendship.

The biggest grouper, which weighed about a hundred pounds, we named Ali Baba; the next, at seventy-five pounds, was Sinbad, and the smallest—only about forty pounds—was Aladdin. I have already remarked that they had different personalities, and this statement often surprises people who cannot imagine that fish, like human beings, are individuals. The middle sized Sinbad was by far the boldest and most aggressive, and often made a nuisance of himself by trying to steal fish we had shot for our own meals. (*We* had to eat, too.) The most striking personality, however, was little Aladdin; he was astonishingly intelligent, and never ceased to amuse us by his display of almost human emotions—especially impatience and jealousy.

It took the groupers only a few demonstrations to learn (a) that Rodney's speargun was much better at catching fish than they were and (b) that if they behaved themselves, they would be rewarded by a free meal. Once we had got this lesson across—and very few land animals would have learned so quickly—we were able to get down to the serious business of taking still and movie photos of our three actors. During the course of about a dozen visits, we were able to record some extraordinary examples of grouper intelligence; indeed, we would hardly have believed our own eyes, if we did not have films to confirm what we saw.

Since Rodney had to do all the work of training—and feeding—our three unusual actors, I cannot do better than quote his own words on the subject:

As soon as we arrived on the "set," which was the seaward end of the Great Basses Reef adjoining a beautiful cave, at least two of our stars would be there to greet us. Usually Ali Baba swam up from the cave, which he regarded as his own private castle, while Sinbad had already joined us from his own territory a few yards to the lee. Aladdin was last on the scene, and usually performed his actions after the larger two had had their fill. It was because of this that he displayed such amusing actions of haste, jealousy and peevishness.

My job was to shoot a fish with a speargun and start the action; long before I had loaded the gun underwater, one of the groupers would stand by expectantly, a few feet from me and literally "point" for me. As the gun was discharged it would alert itself, and make a wild dash for the struggling fish. If I missed (which was fairly often), the expression of bewilderment displayed by the disappointed grouper was remarkable.

If the bait-fish was hit by the harpoon, it was rushed by one or two of the groupers close by, and I had to be very watchful and active to retrieve it. Most often I failed, and one or other of the groupers grabbed the bait, harpoon and all, and made straight for a cave. Then would start a tussle between either Ali Baba or Sinbad or myself. Playing tug-of-war with a hundred pound grouper underwater, even with an aqualung on, is a little one-sided. But thanks to the strong line, I eventually got hold of the harpoon and jerked it free, together with mangled fish, from the cavernous mouth. This took place three or four times per bait-fish, until the grouper decided that the harpoon was not intended for his digestion. Once, in the excitement, Ali Baba took harpoon, bait, and my hand in one quick gulp, and thanks to a tough cloth glove, my wrist was not badly bruised by his numerous small teeth.

Another time Sinbad was so desperate that he opened his mouth extra wide and took in too generous a section of the harpoon which had impaled a small Rudder-fish. This resulted in the harpoon head piercing his lower jaw, bending at right angles, and causing him considerable pain. He changed color with distress, spat out everything in great disgust, and sulked in the cavern for at least twenty minutes while Mike and I wasted precious air trying to reassure him. Eventually he calmed down and even took the bait by swimming slowly, ever so slowly, through a red hula hoop held in my hand.

After removing a fish from the harpoon (a process which was always a little ticklish with one or more hungry groupers waiting to pounce on it), the next step was to feed them, and do it slowly and ostentatiously enough for the still and movie cameras. With one grouper I could always manage, but with two it was impossible; as I hid the fish behind my back after flaunting it before a grouper's face and luring him close, the other would rush in from behind and steal it. Once Sinbad did this with such vigour that he strained my right hand and gulped part of my aqualung harness down with the fish. In shark-infested waters, and with all my attention concentrated on Ali Baba in front of me, this was quite a nerve-shattering experience. After the lung harness had been released, I found that the attack had left a small bruise on my right side.

Petting the groupers could always be done as soon as they had taken a fish from my hand and soon they actually stayed still to be stroked once their appetites had been satisfied. Ali Baba liked being petted most of all, Sinbad did not quite mind, but Alladin was too nippy and impatient for this sort of treatment.

If anyone had told me, before I visited the Great Basses, that groupers could express indignation, disappointment, jealousy and impatience, I would have laughed it off. But I was soon to observe unmistakable emotions such as these, displayed by all three of them, but mainly Aladdin. Once, when I was unduly slow in loading the gun and shooting a passing fish for them, Aladdin sidled up to me, looked me in the face, then made a half rush to a passing blue caranx and actually nodded at it. I obliged by transfixing it and all the while Mike was an incredulous spectator with his Rolleimarine. Then again both Sinbad and Ali Baba had been fed and only Aladdin was hungry. He gave vent to his disappointment by swimming straight up to my speargun while it lay on the bottom and giving the reel an impatient bite!

The culmination of our fraternizing with groupers was the hula hoop act. The idea was to make each grouper in turn swim through a hula hoop with a bait in front of it. We soon found that when they were very hungry the action was too frantic for any camera, still or movie. But with a *hors d'oeuvre* already inside, Ali Baba or Sinbad would oblige with ponderous grace while Mike joyfully filmed the action.

Matador-like, I had to perform all the motions of the bull ring to prevent the bait from being gulped down, yet keep the grouper swimming through the ring and close enough to me for the camera. Ali Baba turned out to be our best hula hoop exponent, but after a particularly try-ing sequence, when Mike never seemed to get enough footage, he got quite sulky and retired into the cave. I pleaded with Mike underwater and at last, when his film was exhausted he gave me the nod. Ali Baba had to be followed deep into his cavern and cajoled into taking his lunch, a caranx all of fifteen pounds. At last he did, but could not swallow it all at once—and he lumbered away into the gloom with the tail protruding grotesquely through his jaws.

The behavior of the three groupers, and the shark attacks, Mike was able to record on color film which he later cut into a remarkable little movie for the Ceylon Tea Propaganda Board, *Beneath the Seas of Ceylon.* This has now been screened and shown on TV in many countries, and its pro-duction—though we certainly never dreamed so at the time— was an important stepping stone to much bigger things. It is strange to realize that meeting Ali Baba, Aladdin, and Sinbad changed our entire lives; though whether for better or worse, we still do not know.

When the *Pharos* returned for us at the end of the week, we departed sunburned and satisfied. We arrived back in Colombo in the nick of time; Mike had been complaining about a stomachache for some days, but it was nothing of the sort. It was acute appendicitis, and he was operated upon with only a few hours to spare.

We had been so busily photographing the groupers, sharks and other local inhabitants of the reef that we had done practically no sightseeing, and had certainly not gone looking for wrecks—though we knew that many must exist in so dangerous an area. As we sailed back to the mainland with the storm clouds of the southwest monsoon already gathering on the horizon, we would have laughed had anyone told us that all the time we had been diving within half a mile of treasure.

Just before we left, I snapped Mike on the gallery of the lighthouse, a hundred feet above the sea, looking out thoughtfully across the reef. The result was a good portrait of the reef, though a poor one of Mike; and by a strange coincidence he was looking almost directly at the site of the treasure wreck—two years ahead in his future, and four years in mine.

5

Boy Beneath the Sea

We bypassed the reef in 1960, because Mike was working for *Time* magazine during the good diving season. He had received an assignment to cover missionary activity in the Borneo jungles, and when there was no trace of him after about five weeks, both we and *Time* assumed that the headhunters had got him. However, he eventually turned up at Bondi Beach, Sydney, among his friends, the Australian surfers; he had decided that, since Australia was practically next door to Borneo, he might as well go back there for a visit. And *Time* got what it wanted; Mike's pictures were in the issue for Easter 1960.

When he returned to the Great Basses Reef in 1961, neither Rodney nor I went with him, to our subsequent regret. Rodney was away on an underwater survey of the Maldive Islands, four hundred miles west of Ceylon. It was here that he made the interesting discovery that, when you are diving at night, there are some inquisitive sharks that will charge straight down the beam of your flashlight. And for my part, I had decided that I was now too old and too fond of com-

fortable living for the rugged sort of existence that one had to
lead on the reef. I was very glad that I had been there, but
had no intention of risking my neck again on those barnacle-
encrusted rocks.

In any case, Mike managed very well without us. He took
with him two young Americans who were first class swimmers
and divers. And when I say young, I mean it. Bobby Kriegel
was fourteen; Mark Smith only thirteen. How Mike had managed to persuade their parents—members of the official
United States community in Ceylon—to let the boys accom-
pany him on such an expedition, I will never know.

But he had it all worked out. He had decided to film an
underwater fantasy about a little boy—Mark—who dreams
that he's exploring the sea—and wakes up to find that his
dream has come true. Mike had written a script not only for
Mark, but also for Ali Baba, Sinbad, and Aladdin. He was
quite confident that they would still be in their cave, and
would do just what he told them when he arrived back on the
scene with his cameras, after his two year absence.

Mark and Bobby were practically amphibious; they spent
all their spare time in the water. We would often meet them
cycling down to the sea, with their spearfishing gear tied to
their bicycles—and see them coming back with fish draped
across their handlebars. They were a complete contrast; Mark
was very small built and blond, looking much younger than
his thirteen years, while Bobby was big and husky. And
whereas Mark had just one sister, Bobby was one of a large
and handsome family that never stayed still long enough to
be counted.

However, both were remarkably mature for their years,
and were extremely anxious to use the aqualung. On their
very first lesson in the local swimming pool, they were able to
throw all their equipment—masks, fins, weightbelt and aqualung—into the water, dive down, and put it all on again before coming to the surface.

They talked very little, but when they did say something, it was always constructive. This does not mean that they were solemn and serious—indeed, they were full of high spirits—but they realized that diving requires care and concentration. After a very few lessons, Mike was confident that they could tackle all ordinary underwater jobs quite safely, and wouldn't lose their heads in an emergency.

The three explorers set off from Colombo in our Volkswagen Microbus loaded with diving gear, and that was the last we heard of them for almost two weeks, except for a brief "All well" message flashed one night by Morse from the lighthouse. There was no telephone from Colombo to Kirinda, so we did not expect any real news of the expedition until it returned.

It was a great relief to everybody when, late one afternoon, Mike and the boys arrived back safely and started unloading the bus. When I asked them eagerly, "Well, how did it go?" they avoided a straight answer, but mumbled something like "Oh, not so badly," as they staggered into my office carrying a battered tin trunk.

On the outward trip, that trunk had contained our cameras; it seemed much heavier now, but I thought nothing of it until Mike locked the office door and said mysteriously: "Look at this."

He threw open the lid—and there were two beautiful little brass cannon, badly worn but gleaming brilliantly where the sea had polished them, and obviously very old. I cried out in excitement: "You've found an old wreck!" Like all divers, we'd been dreaming of this for years, but had never taken the idea very seriously.

Then, without saying a word, Mike lifted the guns and showed me what lay underneath them. At first, I thought I was looking at dirty lumps of coral, about the size of coconuts. Then I realized just what those lumps were; and I was too astonished to say anything.

It was one of the unforgettable moments of a lifetime, for
I knew then that I was staring at something that very few
men have ever seen—genuine, honest-to-goodness treasure.
These unimpressive looking lumps were masses of coins—
hundreds of them, cemented together. When I bent down to
pick one up, I could hardly lift it. It was not—alas!—heavy
enough for gold, but it could only be the next best thing—
silver.

Besides these big lumps, there were hundreds of loose
coins. Many were badly corroded, but most of them seemed
to be in remarkably good condition. They were covered with
Persian lettering, and the total weight of silver came to about
one hundred and fifteen pounds. "But," said Mike, "there's a
lot more where we found this."

In addition to the coins and the little cannon, the expedition had recovered some small copper bars and about twenty
lead musketballs. Altogether, the salvaged material weighed
about two hundredweight, and it was a major feat to have
recovered it from the seabed, got it safely to the lighthouse,
then to the relief boat and across ten miles of sea, and finally
unloaded it on land—all without anyone seeing it.

That evening, we asked the boys' parents round to our
house; at our request, Mark and Bobby had not breathed a
word about the discovery, though this must have been something of a strain. Then we had the pleasure of watching the
Smiths and the Kriegels do a double take, exactly as I had
done, when they looked into the treasure box and realized
just what it held. During the next few days, we were to grow
accustomed to watching perplexity, wonder, disbelief, and
finally excitement spread across the faces of the few trusted
friends we introduced to the finds, which now rested safely
in a massive wooden chest with a big brass padlock.

That chest had been designed to carry explosives, at a time
when Mike fancied he could build up a business as an underwater demolition expert. (He couldn't, and we are still the

embarrassed owners of a quarter of a ton of submarine blasting gelignite.) I could not help thinking that the chest's new
contents were almost as explosive as the old; what it now held
would undoubtedly change our lives, in ways that it was impossible to predict.

For two years that chest has stood in the corner of my
office, where I can see it when I raise my eyes from the type-
writer; it is in front of me now. At first there was an aura of
unreality about it; I could not quite believe that all this had
actually occurred. I am not an unimaginative person, but I
would never have imagined that anything so improbable
could have happened to us.

From time to time, to reassure myself, I will open the lid,
and look at the evidence with my own eyes. But even with
my eyes shut, a reminder is always there. Out of the chest
wells a curious metallic tang as of iodine and seaweed—not
at all unpleasant. It is now one of the most evocative smells
I know; for the rest of my life it will bring back vivid memories of the sea, and of spray-drenched rocks glistening beneath the equatorial sun.

It is the scent of treasure.

6

The Finding

of the Treasure

The other day, I came across Mark Smith's diary of the expedition; it's so brief, and so tantalizing, that I would like to quote it in full. The first entry says simply: *"March 12, 1961. Arrived."*

That one word covers the 175-mile drive down the beautiful, palm-fringed coast of Ceylon—surely one of the loveliest in the world—past dozens of fishing villages with their picturesque outrigger boats drawn up on the beaches. The journey goes through the ancient port of Galle which, say some historians, may be the Tarshish of the Bible—and beyond that into a lonely landscape of still lagoons and patches of jungle. You may meet wild elephants here, but they seldom bother motorists.

At Kirinda, the jumping-off point for the reef, Mike and the boys unloaded all their gear, and by next day had recovered somewhat. *"March 13. Surfed all day—in late afternoon repacked gear."*

They went to bed early that night, because the *Pharos* would leave at 4 A.M., when the sea was at its calmest. The ten mile journey to the lighthouse, the giddy trip up the swaying rope, and the transfer of tons of equipment from pitching boat to the spray-drenched rocks at the base of the great tower, Mark sums up as follows: *"March 14.   Left for G.B. Stowed gear, etc."*

Having been through all this myself, I am not in the least surprised that he had no energy to write any more. But by the next morning operations were in full swing, and Mark becomes positively garrulous. I will give the rest of his diary without a break:

> *March 15.*   Sea bad, strong current, big chop. No SCUBA diving, snorkeled. Met Sinbad and Ali Baba, regained friendship.
> *March 16.*   Took first SCUBA dive. Saw and filmed groupers, Mike saw barracuda, big shark.
> *March 17.*   Sea good, took two dives. 1st. Filmed Sinbad and Ali Baba. 2nd. Saw dozen tunas, from 75 to 200 pounds. Had big giant grouper (300 pounds) chase us. Took stills of caves, batfish and groupers. Bobby saw same (?) big shark as seen yesterday (10 ft.).

This was not a bad beginning for any underwater expedition; after that, however, things got too hectic for Mark to continue his literary activities. Fortunately, we have a full account of what happened next, for as soon as they returned to the mainland, I interviewed both boys with a tape recorder, while their impressions were still sharp and clear. So in what follows, I am able to give their actual words, spoken while they were still gripped by the excitement of the discovery.

For the next four days, they continued diving and filming. They would jump off the rugged, barnacle-encrusted edge of the reef and swim out to the groupers' home, about a hundred yards away, towing a large inflated inner tube from which the aqualungs and cameras were hung. If the currents were against them, this could be very hard work; it sometimes took half an hour to cover this short distance.

After anchoring the float, they would put on their lungs and dive down to the bottom, where the groupers would at once greet them with open mouths. Sometimes, if they were not fed immediately, they would become impatient, and on one occasion a greedy Sinbad swallowed Mark's arm up to the elbow. As the grouper was more than twice his size, there was nothing that Mark could do but wait until he got his arm back. Fortunately, groupers have very small teeth, and the incident left only a few scars which Mark displayed proudly until they healed. Perhaps it was lucky that nothing like this happened with the *really* big grouper seen on March 17—an unfriendly character who was left strictly alone.

Then, on March 22—but let Bobby Kriegel tell you the story in his own words, as taken down on the tape recorder:

Well, the sea was unusually calm; in fact, it was so calm that there was no current to take away the sand in the water. So it wasn't very clear and we couldn't get any pictures. That day, some porpoises came unusually close, about fifty feet away from the lighthouse, and Mike, Mark and I set off to see how close we could get to them. We saw them and when they disappeared, we went away. Since there was no tide and we couldn't take any pictures, we decided to go down and explore one of the reefs which had never been seen underwater. So we went down there and on the way Mike told us later that he thought he saw a cannonball. Then we saw a small cannon, about two and one-half feet long. Mike dived down—no, Mike didn't dive down to it. He showed it to me and pointed. I dived down and tried to pull it up. I couldn't do it. So then Mike dived down and lifted it free, then put it back down. Mike said that the wreck might have hit on one side of the reef and some more might be on the other side; so we swam round the edge of it.

After we got to the other side the first thing we saw was a shiny cannon, about two and one-half feet long, sitting on the edge of a big canyon; and it was worn smooth by the water, and shining as though someone had put it there the other day.

These two little cannon (their correct name is "swivel guns"), had been polished by the waves and the sand until their brass gleamed like gold. From a distance, indeed, they looked brand new. They were the unmistakable signposts without which the wreck might never have been discovered. We now think that they must have been well up on the tall stern of the ship, and fell on the higher part of the reef when she went aground. They had been lying there for centuries, rolling back and forth in the swell which surges almost continually across the reef in bad weather and in good, waiting for Mike to spot them.

It is nearly always the cannon that betray an old wreck. When the hull decays and collapses—which takes only a few years—they remain intact. Even when they become completely covered with coral, their straight lines are an immediate give-away, for nothing natural in the sea is perfectly straight.

But back to Mike and the boys—

They were a long way from the lighthouse—more than a thousand feet, which was a tremendous distance, even for a good swimmer, against the powerful currents that sweep along the reef. And they had no aqualungs, no underwater cameras—for, after all, they had merely been on a sightseeing trip. So they decided that the best thing to do was to go back to the lighthouse, have lunch, and return properly equipped in the afternoon.

After a hasty meal, they were back on the site with their aqualungs and the big inner tube. Now they were able to make a more thorough investigation, and slowly the pattern of the wreck began to emerge. The hull had been smashed to pieces, and no trace of it was left. In fact, ninety nine skindivers out of a hundred would have swum right over the site without seeing a thing—except for one cannon, about five feet long, which lay on the seabed like the fallen column from some Greek temple. Not far from it were shapeless mounds which, on more careful inspection, turned out to be two huge anchors tangled together. And near what must have been the middle of the ship was a pile of about a dozen large iron cannon, jumbled together like matchsticks split from a box.

It was that afternoon, on their second dive, that they made the big discovery that turned this from another old wreck to something even more exciting. Listen to Mark Smith's rather breathless account, which I think conveys the drama of that moment very well:

> We took out the big inner tube and were going to take out the filming equipment, but Bob drifted down the current so fast that Mike put the film equipment away and we went out with aqualungs. Then, when we got near the spot, we turned on our aqualungs and went down and Mike was hitting everything he saw with his knife. Then Mike came over to us and showed us the cannon, and Bob pointed out something shining right near it. Mike examined it and said it was silver, underwater with his mouthpiece on!

Both boys were much impressed by this last feat. It is virtually impossible to talk underwater when you are gripping an aqualung mouthpiece between your teeth; but Mike yelled "Silver!" so loudly that they both heard him.

Then the hunt was on; listen to Mark again:

> Then we all three started to uncover the sand. We pushed it away and then we saw all the coins stuck to the rock. So we started working on the coins and that day we got a small bag full of loose coins and a few little

pieces of coral with coins in it. Then we took it back to the lighthouse at the time that the lighthouse keepers were taking a nap. . .

Already the little expedition was up against the problem that would give us one of our biggest headaches in the future —security. They could not guess the importance of this find, but it was obviously wise to keep it secret for the present. There were four lighthouse men with them on the rock, and if the news got back to land there was always a possibility that someone else might come out and clean up the wreck. We were not the only divers in Ceylon.

While the lighthouse staff was still having its afternoon siesta, continues Mark:

> We spread all the treasure out and the two cannon that we'd got, and Mike photographed them. We put the silver inside a kit bag, but we didn't show the lighthouse keepers the treasure, though we showed them the two cannon that we'd got. The next day, early morning, the water was still not clear around the lighthouse, so we went out to the wreck—this time with all the equipment —knives, crowbars, chisels, and the big inner tube. This time we also took the still cameras. We went off to the place and this time we got a lot of bags full of loose coins and some chunks of silver coins. Then we went back to the lighthouse and that afternoon we spent our time chipping out the coins and washing them. The next morning, we went out and got the big hunks of silver coins—four big lumps and some loose ones. And that was the last time we went out to the wreck; we paddled back to the lighthouse and squared everything away.

The underwater photographs that Mike took on these two trips are, as far as I know, the only ones ever made showing treasure at the actual moment of recovery from the seabed.

We have kept them secret for over two years, but we do not mind publishing them now; for this section of the reef looks quite different today, thanks to the hard work done by our latest expedition.

Altogether, Mike and the boys spent only two days diving on the wreck, without proper equipment, and with no boat. Yet they brought back some two hundred pounds of material —including the two little swivel guns, which weigh about thirty pounds each. As the swim to the lighthouse often took more than an hour, this was a really astonishing performance. Now that I have visited the site myself, I am still more amazed at what they accomplished.

Then the water became clear again, and they continued with the movie making—which is what they had come to do in the first place. Mike took the final shots of his fantasy, showing Mark swimming slowly through the blue-green valleys of the reef while Sinbad, Aladdin, and Ali Baba escort him like three friendly dogs. Mark turns to wave goodby to them as they drop behind; to us now, that gesture has a special poignancy. For none of us would ever see the groupers again; that was the end of our three-year partnership.

Next year, some foreign "sportsmen" who had seen Mike's movies and stills, and had heard rumors of the treasure, went out to the reef. They had no difficulty, of course, in spearing Sinbad, Ali Baba, and Aladdin, when they swam up to them trustfully, expecting to be fed.

But the brave hunters did not find the wreck.

7

Mogul Silver

The first order of business was, clearly, to identify the coins, in the hope that we could discover the wreck's nationality and origin. We were also, quite naturally, interested in their value; though a hundredweight of silver was obviously not to be sneered at, old coins are always worth more than their mere weight in bullion.

The coins that Mike and the boys had brought back could be divided into three groups. Most of them were cemented together in twenty-five or thirty pound lumps; where one of these had been split open, it was obvious that the coins inside it were in absolutely perfect condition, looking as if they had come straight from the mint. Others were in smaller lumps, where anything up to a dozen had been concreted together and partly overgrown with coral; here again, the coins in the middle were often in excellent condition. The rest were loose specimens, which had been scattered in hundreds over the seabed. Most of these were badly wasted—many being mere wafers of corrosion products that could never have been identified as coins except by chemical analysis; all the silver had been converted into silver sulphide, which is the normal fate of this metal in the sea.

We sorted out a few dozen of the best specimens, and cleaned them up in battery acid, which dissolved away the remaining traces of coral. Now the handsome Persian script was perfectly legible; and so was the date.

Every coin was clearly marked with the same number, consisting of three 1's followed by a sign that looks like a 1 attached to a little 3 lying on its back. This is in fact the Arabic 3, so the date was 1113.

We knew that the Muslim world dates its calendar not from the birth of Christ, as we do,[1] but from the Hegira, the day when Mohammed fled from Mecca, which was July 16, 622 A.D. So we innocently added 622 to 1113 and arrived at 1735 A.D. This was completely wrong, and is a good example of the dangers facing amateur archeologists. For the Muslim year is not the same as ours; to the Arabs, in their clear, desert climate, the phases of the moon are of vital importance and their calendar is, therefore, a lunar, not solar, one, containing either 354 or 355 days. So the Muslim and Christian years get out of step at the rate of about three years in every century, and 1113 A.H. is *not* 1735 A.D., but 1702 A.D.

When we made cautious inquiries of local numismatists, we found that our coins were rupees from the year 45 in the reign of the Mogul emperor Aurangzeb, who held sway over much of India from 1658 to 1707 A.D. They had been minted at Surat, in northwest India, and were the common currency of a large area of Asia in the eighteenth century. The ship carrying them need not have come direct from India, but the fact that all the coins appeared to be brand new, *and all bore the same date*,[2] certainly made this appear likely.

We soon made another interesting discovery. When we weighed the cemented coin masses, and calculated how many

---

[1] Actually, we don't; according to most authorities, Jesus Christ was born in 4 B.C. Our calendar has been four years out ever since the sixth century!

[2] We have since found *one*—just one among all the thousands—bearing the date 1096 (i.e. 1685 A.D.). Perhaps it was not part of the main consignment, but a loose coin belonging to one of the crew.

coins they contained, the answers came out to almost exactly
1,000. It was obvious what had happened; the coins had been
packed in bags of 1,000, which had been sealed after counting. (Later, we were to find pieces of sacking from these
bags.) When the ship had gone down, the bags had lasted
long enough for the outer layers of rupees to become cemented together by the action of the sea. Thus those inside
the lump were perfectly preserved, while the whole mass re-
tained the shape of the original bag.

When we read accounts of other treasure discoveries, we
were interested to see how often this happens. Perhaps the
most successful treasure hunt of all time was that of William
Phips on the Silver Shoals, north of Haiti, where a Spanish
galleon carrying an enormous cargo of silver went down in
1641. Captain Phips led a salvage fleet to the area in 1687,
and recovered coins and bullion to the value of about $700,-
000 (several millions in today's money). Here is an account,
by an eyewitness, of the treasure as it was hauled in:

> And so the dollars they hoisted in by whole chests of
> 2,000 dollars together, for although the chests were rot-
> ted off and consumed, yet the dollars, with rust, were so
> grown together that they hung together as one lump—
> although the middlemost of the chest was bright and
> sound—and not many of them was much wasted by the
> water.

This was the state of the treasure only forty-six years after
it had sunk; ours was in exactly the same condition 260 years
later.

All this strongly suggested that we were dealing with a
new consignment that had come straight from the mint of
Surat. Perhaps our wreck had been a government ship, bringing currency to Ceylon to pay for the many expenses of ad-
ministration. Or perhaps she was a trader plying on the Spice
Route, carrying what was known as "Silk Money" to pay for
her purchases.

We knew very little about the history of Ceylon and India
in 1702, but we started learning fast. It was a period when the
British, Dutch, and Portuguese were all jockeying for position in the East, laying the foundations of the empires whose
disintegration we have just witnessed in our own time.

In Ceylon, the Dutch were in power—at least, in the low-
lying coastal regions; the Sinhalese were still masters of the
central mountains, and would continue to be for a hundred
years, until the British conquered the country. Our first guess
was that the wreck had been one of the ships of the Dutch
East India Company—that extraordinary trading organiza-
tion, with its own army and navy, which ruled much of the
East like an independent sovereign state.

In the subcontinent of India, the cruel and brilliant reign
of the Mogul emperors was drawing to its close. Aurangzeb
was the last great name in the glittering sequence: Babur—
Akbar—Jahangir—Shah Jahan—names which can still stir
the blood across the centuries. Though only the third in suc-
cession of Shah Jahan's sons, Aurangzeb was much the most
able, and while his father was still alive, defeated his three
brothers in the usual dispute for the throne. For the last eight
years of his life Shah Jahan was imprisoned, not uncomfort-
ably, in Agra, the city where he had built the world's most
magnificent tomb for his wife Mumtaz Mahal, Aurangzeb's
mother.

To have ruled India for fifty years was an amazing achieve-
ment, yet for all his political cunning, Aurangzeb left a herit-
age of chaos. He was a religious fanatic and tried to impose
strict Muslim ritual upon a largely Hindu population. The result, as it must always be, was a hostile and finally rebellious
country. Soon after the old emperor's death in 1707, India
disintegrated into the civil wars which paved the way for the
Western invaders.

In Aurangzeb's time, British merchants—in the form of the
East India Company of London—were already well established in India, though they had been foolish enough to en-

gage in one brief and unsuccessful war with the emperor (1685-87) which had resulted in their temporary expulsion. But they came back, and indeed at this date when our coins were minted *two* rival British East India companies were functioning—to the confusion of Aurangzeb and the profit of his ministers, who took bribes from both sides with great impartiality.

Aurangzeb died five years after the date shown on our coins; when they were minted, he was already a weary old man of eighty-four, worn down by ceaseless military campaigns and religious austerities. Few despots can have possessed so much power and obtained so little satisfaction from it. The bigotry which destroyed his empire also corroded his soul, and his faith did not give him the consolation one feels he should have earned. Reading the letters he wrote to his sons on his deathbed, who would wish to change places with the first man ever to rule the whole of India?

> I know not who I am, where I shall go, or what will happen to this sinner full of sins. Now I will say good-bye to everyone in this world. . . . My famous and auspicious sons should not quarrel among themselves and allow a general massacre of the people. . . . My years have gone by profitless. . . . There is no hope for me in the future. . . . I have greatly sinned and know not what torment awaits me. . . ."[3]

Aurangzeb's plea to his sons was, of course, futile. As he had fought his own brothers, so they fought among themselves. And presently, to their great surprise, the British found themselves the masters of India. There was no one else to run it.

---

[3] See *The Oxford History of India* (V. A. Smith), chapter on Aurangzeb.

Fig. 1. The Great Basses lighthouse, photographed one month after the 1963 expedition. The wreck site is a quarter of a mile to the left.

Fig. 2. The skyline at Kirinda, showing the shrine.

Fig. 3. Air view of Kirinda, showing the shrine from which the reef operations were observed and photographed. The Great Basses Reef is on the horizon but invisible.

Royal Ceylon Air Force

Fig. 4. The Tangalle coast, looking westward.

Fig. 5. Hauling in boat at Kirinda.

Fig. 6. Peter does some appropriate reading while relaxing at Kirinda.

Fig. 7. Kirinda villagers listen to their tape-recorded songs.

Fig. 8. Hector has second thoughts about diving.

Fig. 9. Ceylon rope trick; Hector pumping up aqualungs.

Fig. 10. Passing the Great Basses; Mike and Elizabeth aboard *Via Vida*.

Fig. 11. From the Ramparts of Galle, Mike and Peter plan new conquests.

Fig. 12. Elephant at Yala.

Fig. 13. Mike (left) racing *Pegasus*.

Royal Ceylon Air Force

Fig. 14. The Great Basses Reef. Shark Tooth Rock visible above breakers on far right.

Fig. 15. The Little Basses lighthouse. What wrecks remain to be discovered in this completely unexplored territory?

Royal Ceylon Air Force

Fig. 16. *Ran Muthu* loading, Colombo; Martin aboard.

Fig. 17. *Ran Muthu* loading, Tangalle; Martin rows dinghy to boat.

Fig. 18. Tangalle resthouse; Martin brings ashore the broken exhaust.

Fig. 19. Our hotel; inside the boat shed, Kirinda.

Fig. 20. Carrying down the dinghy, Kirinda Beach.

Fig. 21. Loading the dinghy, Kirinda; the little girl doesn't want her photo taken.

Fig. 22. The Great Basses Reef; Shark's Tooth Rock in center.

Fig. 23. A rough launch; Peter tries to protect the loud-hailer.

Fig. 24. The Great Basses lighthouse; coast of Ceylon in background.

Fig. 25. Mike on the lighthouse gallery, showing complete vista of the reef and the wreck site. Shark's Tooth Rock at center.

Mike Wilson

Fig. 26. Dinghy on station above divers; Laza watches out for breakers.

Fig. 27. Divers returning to boat with finds.

Fig. 28. Too rough for diving!

Fig. 29. The beginning of the adventure; dwarfed by the surrounding ships *Ran Muthu* leaves Colombo Harbor.

Mike Wilson

Fig. 30. A rough day on the reef; photographed from sea level on the lighthouse.

Fig. 31. Kirinda Beach.

8

What To Do

Till the Lawyers Come

All these thousands of new 1702 rupees were a very strong indication that our unknown ship had sunk not long after that date—perhaps even in the same year, if she had come directly from Surat. It was easy to picture some unfortunate merchant or East India Company official making a large cash withdrawal of brand new coins from the mint, then sailing straight to disaster.

However, there was no reason to suppose that the ship had touched at Ceylon, or was heading there. If she were British, she would be avoiding the island, as the Dutch were in control; perhaps she was bound on company business from the West to the East coast of India. And even if she were Dutch, she might have been sailing directly to Batavia or other East Indian trading posts. Ships on this route often carried very large consignments of coins; we have a record of one sailing from Surat to Batavia in 1703 with almost half a million rupees aboard.

Yet it was equally possible that the ship had had dealings with Ceylon, which was a clearinghouse for currency—and

was often chronically short of silver. In this connection, a
historian friend of ours, Major R. Raven-Hart, made a very
intriguing discovery. While translating a German book about
Ceylon (*The Wandering Swabian*, Martin Wintergerst,
Memmingen, 1712), Major Raven-Hart came across this
passage: "On July 16 (1706) arrived at Trincomalee. . . .
our Master applied for two months pay for us to the Commander. He said that if we would accept copper coins he
would pay us; we agreed to this."

Why was silver so scarce in Trincomalee in 1706? Could
that have anything to do with our wreck, just a few years
before? But one could speculate endlessly; we needed more
facts—and that meant going back to the Reef, which we
could not do for another year.

We were trapped in something of a vicious circle. A properly equipped expedition would be expensive, and we could
not risk it unless we were sure of the financial outcome. Yet
until we did return to the wreck, we would not know what
it held.

I tried to clarify the situation by examining the underwater photographs that Mike had taken, and quizzing the
boys, but the results were more tantalizing than instructive.
For example:

CLARKE   What area would you say the coins covered,
   how big an area?

KRIEGEL   Well, the coins are at the bottom, next to the
   cannon—covering about five feet long and say up to
   two feet wide. Then if you went along a side of the
   wall, I'd say it would have got down to six feet long
   and still about two, two-and-a-half feet wide. But this
   wall was perpendicular to the bottom of the sand, so
   if it was laid over flat, it would probably be three feet
   wide.

CLARKE   You mean there were some coins in this wall?

KRIEGEL On the surface of the wall we could see there were coins and knocked three or four hunks off this wall; I mean by hunks about a thousand coins stuck together.

CLARKE Well, those are quite sizable lumps because I've calculated that one of those twenty-five pound lumps does contain just about a thousand coins. And you mean to say that this wall was really made of lumps of coins?

KRIEGEL Well, it seemed to be. As far as we could see, it was made of lumps of coins.

A wall of silver was certainly an exciting prospect, but I did not take it too seriously, because I appreciated the extreme difficulty of making accurate observations underwater. Nevertheless, it would be very surprising if, after only two days of work, the boys had recovered more than a small fraction of the coins present. Their five thousand or so rupees might be a drop in the bucket, and my thoughts went back to that Surat-Batavia Dutchman carrying half a million. A rough calculation showed that this would amount to about *five tons* of silver; we would be very happy to settle for even one.

A new expedition seemed a good risk, but we needed some assurance that we could keep the treasure if we found it. The very day that Mike got back with the silver, he called in his lawyer and we started looking into the legal situation. Our first thought was that it was "treasure trove," and we were surprised to learn that it was nothing of the sort. For "treasure trove" consists of valuables hidden *in the land,* with the intention of recovering them again; on both counts, this ruled out coins lost in the sea.

The next problem was a knottier one; had we found the treasure in Ceylon, or outside it? All countries bordering the sea claim certain rights over a band known as territorial waters, which usually extends from three miles beyond low tide. Some countries, including Ceylon, claim six miles; others claim even more, and there have been endless international arguments over this.

Our wreck was *just* outside the six mile limit; so, as the first finders, we could maintain that it belonged to us and to no one else. But the matter wasn't as simple as that; every time we thought that one point had been settled, another turned up.

Though we considered that we had found this silver on (or under) the high seas, we had certainly brought it *into* Ceylon when we came ashore. Today, every country has, alas, elaborate import regulations; you cannot bring anything across a border without filling in many forms, and usually, paying some duty. But to our pleased surprise, we found that there was no duty on silver, so we had not been technically guilty of smuggling. Nevertheless, to make certain that there would be no trouble later, we showed all our finds to the customs authorities, who confirmed that they had no legal interest in the matter.

A few weeks later, we re-exported one of the coin masses, together with a few loose coins, to the Smithsonian Institution in Washington. The Smithsonian's Curator of Armed Services History, Mendel Peterson, is a sort of one-man clearinghouse for information on wrecks, and has built up a fine display of salvaged material. His advice had been of great assistance to us, and we felt that the least we could do was to donate one of our samples for exhibition. This would have several valuable secondary effects; it would authenticate the wreck, help to focus interest on Ceylon, and give many readers of this book a chance of seeing some of the treasure, if they ever happen to be in Washington.[1]

---

[1] The lump donated is the one at the upper right-hand of Fig. 48. It is Number 239761 in the acquisition list of the Smithsonian Institution, which has valued it at $2,500.

We spent over a whole year, and a considerable amount of money, in vain attempts to discover who, if anyone, actually owned the treasure. As far as Ceylon was concerned, it appeared that there was simply no definite law on the subject. We were doing something for the first time, and there were no precedents to guide us. Our proctor, one of the keenest legal minds in the country, would descend upon me every week or so with a whole library of law volumes, which usually had the effect of leaving me in a state of utter confusion. I will do my best to pass on some of this confusion with interest.

The Ceylon legal system is a legacy of the Dutch, modified by the British during the one hundred and fifty years of their occupation, and by the Ceylonese after they achieved independence in 1947. In general, however, the law administered in Ceylon regarding maritime and salvage matters is English law, unless any provision to the contrary has been made. But at this point, I cannot do better than to quote from a memorandum prepared by our energetic proctor, Homi Rustomjee, in which he set out all that he had discovered in his researches. It gives an excellent summary of the complications involved—though I will warn you right away that I am leaving the most important of them all until a later chapter. This is merely the first installment.

The Roman Dutch Law recognises a form of acquiring ownership of property by a method known as *occupatio* which is defined as the lawful seizing (with the intention of becoming owner) of an unowned corporeal thing capable of ownership and is applicable, inter alia, to abandoned things (*res derelictae*) and to every ownable thing which either never has been owned or having been owned once is owned no longer.—*Professor R. W. Lee: Introduction to Roman Dutch Law.*

The position is the same under *English Common Law.*

Treasure Trove is where any gold or silver in coin, plate, or bullion is found concealed in a house, or in the earth, or other private place, the owner thereof being unknown, in which case the treasure belongs to the King or his grantee, having the franchise of treasure trove. . . . If the owner, instead of hiding the treasure, casually lost it, or purposely parted with it in such a manner that it is evident he intended to abandon the property altogether, and did not propose to resume it on another occasion, or if he threw it on the ground, or other public place, or in the sea, the first finder is entitled to the property as against everyone but the owner, and the King's prerogative does not in this respect obtain. So that it is the hiding, and not the abandonment of the property that entitles the King to it.—*Halsbury's Laws of England-Gratuitous Bailment-Finding of chattels-Chitty on Prerogative page 152—cited by Farwell J in A.G. vs. Trustees of British Museum (1903) 2 Ch. 598 at 608. See also A. G. vs. Moore (1893) 1 Ch. 676.*

The Crown gains no title unless the treasure is actually hidden in the earth with the *animus revocandi.* Therefore where it is scattered in the sea or on the surface of the earth, or lost or abandoned, it belongs to the first finder.—*Halsbury's Laws of England-Constitutional Law Section—The Revenues of the Crown-Treasure Trove.*

The Civil Law Ordinance No: 5 of 1852 stated that the law to be administered in Ceylon in respect of salvage and generally to maritime matters shall be the English Law unless other provision is or shall be made by any Ordinance now in force in Ceylon *or hereafter to be enacted.*

Thereafter the *Wrecks and Salvage Ordinance No: 5*

of 1861 was enacted. The title to the Ordinance states that it is an ordinance relating to wrecks, Sea Casualties and Salvage *within the limits of Ceylon.*

The Ordinance referred to above states that a *"wreck"* includes jetsam, flotsam, lagan, and *derelict* found in or on *the shores of the sea* or *any tidal water.*

Section 3 sets out the duties of a receiver of wrecks in respect of a ship or boat which is stranded or in distress at any place on the shores of the sea or of any tidal water *within the limits of Ceylon.*

Section 12 sets out the rules to be observed by any person finding or taking possession of a wreck *within Ceylon.* It is the duty of such person to deliver same to the receiver.

Section 17 has above it the heading *Salvage in Ceylon* and deals with the case of a ship or boat which is stranded or otherwise in distress *on the shores of any sea of or tidal water in Ceylon.* It is conceded that such section also refers to the case "whenever any wreck is saved by any person other than a Receiver." But there cannot be the slightest doubt that even such last mentioned case must be within the limits of Ceylon.

Section 27 states that whenever any articles belonging to or forming part of any foreign ship which has been wrecked on or near the coasts of Ceylon or belonging to or forming part of any cargo thereof are found *on or near such coasts* or are brought into any port in Ceylon, the Consul General of the country to which such ship or in the case of the cargo to which the owners of such cargo may have belonged, shall, in the absence of the owner of such ship or articles and of the master and other agent of the owner, be deemed to be the agent of the owner, so far as relates to the custody and disposal of such articles.

Sea Shore is that portion of the land which lies between the high water mark of the ordinary tides and low water mark.

Tidal waters means any part of the sea and any part of a river within the ebb and flow of the tide at ordinary spring tides, and not being a harbor.[2]

Admiralty Jurisdiction—Under Ordinances Nos: 2 of 1891 and 15 of 1893 the Supreme Court of Ceylon is declared to be a Colonial Court of Admiralty and to have jurisdiction, subject to the provisions and limitations contained in the *Colonial Courts of Admiralty Act, 1890* over the like places, persons, matters and things as the Admiralty Jurisdiction of the High Court of England, whether existing by virtue of any Statute or otherwise, and such Colonial Court of Admiralty may exercise such Jurisdiction in like manner and to as full an extent as the High Court in England, and shall have the same regard as that Court to international law and the comity of nations.

It is to be noted that no provision has been made for the application of any subsequent Act after 1890. Could it be maintained that all subsequent legislation passed in England is also applicable to Ceylon in regard to Admiralty matters when the above ordinances do not refer to future legislation or to the legislation from time to time applicable to the Admiralty Jurisdiction of the High Court of England?

The Ceylon Independence Act 1947 states that Sections 4 and 7 of 53 & 54 Victoria Ch. 27 (the Act referred to in Ordinance No: 2 of 1891) and Sections 735 and 736 of the Merchant Shipping Act 57 & 58 Victoria Ch. 60 shall not be applicable to Ceylon.

[2] Unless you are a lawyer, you'll be grinding to a halt about here. So skip if you must—but don't miss the Chinaman and the condensed milk at the end of this chapter.

The position under the Admiralty and Merchant Shipping Acts in England appears to be as follows:

Halsbury's Laws of England-Wreck—Dealing with wreck—*Duties of finders of wrecks*—"A person who finds or takes possession of any wreck within the limits of the United Kingdom, or *any wreck found outside those limits and brought within them,* must, if he is the owner, give notice to the receiver of wrecks for the district of the fact and a description of the marks by which the wreck may be recognised." See also The Liffey (1887) 58 L.T. 351 and The Zeta (1875) L.R. 4 A. & E. 460.

Again, *Halsbury—Volume 1—Page 68, note h:* "As to wrecks found or taken possession of outside the limits of the United Kingdom, and brought within those limits, see *Merchant Shipping Act 1906 (6 Edw 7 ch 48 section 72)."* Also under *Unclaimed wreck:* "The jurisdiction of the High Court of Admiralty to condemn as droits of admiralty unclaimed wreck, flotsam, jetsam, lagan and derelict found on the high seas beyond the limits of the United Kingdom, is now within the limits of the Admiralty jurisdiction of the High Court, but no necessity for the exercise of the jurisdiction can ordinarily arise, as droits of Admiralty in time of peace are dealt with by the Receiver of Wreck of the district or by the Ministry of Transport as Receiver General of Admiralty Droits.

6 Edw 7 Ch. 48 Section 72. It is enacted that section 518 of the Principal Act shall apply to wreck found or taken possession of outside the limits of the United Kingdom, and brought within the limits of the United Kingdom, as it applies to wrecks found or taken possession of within the limits of the United Kingdom.

Section 518 of the Principal Act—Merchant Shipping Acts 1894 to 1900 and the Act 6 Edw 7 Ch. 48—sets out that it is the duty of any person finding wreck or taking possession of wreck within the limits of the United Kingdom, to give notice of finding and hand over the wreck to the Receiver of Wrecks.

So that the position in the United Kingdom since the passing of the Act 6 Edw 7 Ch. 48 is quite clear: Wrecks found outside the limits of the United Kingdom are subject to the same provisions as wrecks found within the limits of the United Kingdom if such wrecks are brought within the limits of the United Kingdom.

The question has to be considered whether the provisions of the Act 6 Edw 7 Ch. 48 apply to Ceylon.

This point came up for decision in the case of *The Yuri Maru* (1927 A.C.906 and 43 T.L.R.698) in which the Privy Council of England considered the jurisdiction of a Colonial Court of Admiralty and decided that a Colonial Court of Admiralty has the same administrative jurisdiction as the High Court of England had at the time of the passing of the Admiralty Act of 1890. The Privy Council held that the extension of the Admiralty Jurisdiction of the High Court of England by the Admiralty Acts of 1920 and 1925 did not apply to a Colonial Court of Admiralty. This view of the Privy Council has been adopted in Ceylon as being one to be followed by the Courts of Admiralty of Ceylon—see *63 New Law Reports at page 343 and 64 New Law Reports page 273.*

The position, then, in Ceylon, would be that wrecks found outside the limits of Ceylon are governed by the provisions of the Admiralty Acts prevailing in England in 1890. Such Acts make no reference to wrecks found outside the limits of the United Kingdom.

It is submitted therefore that wrecks found beyond the limits of Ceylon belong to the finder even though brought within the limits of Ceylon.

In this connection it is to be noted that the entire Merchant Shipping Law of Ceylon is sought to be completely revised and brought up to date by the *Merchant Shipping Act No: 7 of 1953* which states in Section 232 thereof that even wrecks found beyond the limits of Ceylon and brought within such limits have to be delivered to the Receiver of Wrecks. Ceylon, has at long last, sought to bring herself into line with the present law in England. But such *Merchant Shipping Act No: 7 of 1953* has up to date not been proclaimed yet.

That last sentence seemed to leave the whole subject wide open. The act had been drafted—almost ten years ago—but not yet passed! Until it became law, we could argue that anything found in a wreck outside Ceylon definitely belonged to us, and need not be handed over to the authorities. The fact that the Principal Collector of Customs, who was the supervisor of wrecks for Ceylon, had already disclaimed interest in our finds seemed to strengthen this argument.

We were also encouraged to discover a fascinating salvage case which appeared to give us a degree of protection—even if we were compelled to hand over the treasure. This was an action in the Colonial Court of Admiralty of Ceylon, before Chief Justice Basnayake, in which the plaintiff was the Polish Ocean Lines of Gdyina. The very first paragraph is a rich blend of Hammond Innes and Sax Rohmer; here is the complete report of the case:

June 7, 1957. Basnayake, C.J.
This is an action for salvage by the salvor the Polish Ocean Lines of Gdynia in Poland. It would appear that when the plaintiff's motor vessel "Mickiewicsz" of 2,240 tons was proceeding on a voyage from Tsing Tao laden with a cargo of Peanuts and Sesame seeds on or about 2nd April 1953, a motor launch was noticed in the Bay of Bengal about 700 miles from Colombo Latitude 05° 56" N Longitude 91° 45" E adrift in the Ocean. A Chinaman, its sole occupant, was in an exhausted condition. The Master picked up the motor launch with the famished Chinaman. On examination it was found that the launch

had a cargo of 29 packages of tins described as condensed milk which when opened were found to contain opium. The course of the vessel was deviated to Colombo, which was the nearest port. The Customs authorities took charge of the opium which weighed 738 kilograms and was valued at Rs.29,562.71 and the motor launch was taken over by the plaintiff's agent in Colombo, the Ceylon Trading Company Ltd.,

The Attorney-General and the Principal Collector of Customs who were noticed deny any liability to pay salvage to the plaintiff. Neither the owner of the salvaged vessel nor the Chinaman who was found in it has though noticed entered appearance in these proceedings. The Principal Collector of Customs has deposited the value of the opium in Court and neither he nor the Attorney-General makes any claim thereto.

The only question that arises for decision is what amount is the plaintiff entitled to as salvage. There is no absolute rule or fixed scale of remuneration in civil salvage (The Ewell Grove 1835 3 Hagg. 209,221). The amount of the salvor's reward, in the absence of a valid agreement, is a matter to be determined in the discretion of the Court. There are certain limits laid down in the decisions. Kennedy (Civil Salvage 3rd Ed. p. 146) states:—

"It may be taken, however, as a safe general rule that in no case in which the owner of the salvaged property appears will the Court award the salvor more than a moiety of the value of the salvaged property."

The matters that may be taken into account in assessing the reward are thus classified in Kennedy:

A. As regards the things salved:
    (1) The degree of danger to human life.
    (2) The degree of danger to property.
    (3) The value of the property as salved.

B. As regards the salvors:
  (1) The degree of danger to human life.
  (2) Their skill and conduct.
  (3) The value of the property employed in the salvage service.
  (4) The danger to which the property is exposed.
  (5) The time and labour expended in the performance of the salvage service.
  (6) Responsibilities incurred in the performance of the salvage service, such, e.g. as risk to the insurance, and liability to passengers or freighters through deviation or delay.
  (7) Loss or expense incurred in the performance of the salvage service, such, e.g. as detention, loss of profitable trade, or repair or damage caused to ship, boats, or gear.

The amount of the salvage reward depends on how many of the above elements are present in a given case. According to the plaintiff's statement, which is uncontradicted, the costs incurred in the salvage including the deviation is £1,332-7-8. The plaintiff does not state that the salvage itself was hazardous or involved any loss or expense in its performance. It is not alleged that freighters have made any claim on the plaintiff in consequence of the deviation. The plaintiff had also to take the Chinaman to a port that would permit him to land, as the immigration authorities in Colombo refused to admit him. The salvaged launch is valued at Rs.1,000.

There is a further circumstance that has to be taken into account in determining the amount of the reward payable. The launch was a derelict at the time it was salvaged. The practice of the Court of Admiralty in awarding a reward for salvage of a derelict is stated thus by Brett M. R. in *The City of Chester*:[3]

> Even in the case of derelict the Court of Admiralty has hardly ever under any circumstances, and in no known case of non-derelict has ever awarded, as for salvage reward, more than half of the value of the property saved. [Instances of rewards of more than half are not unknown in cases in which the owners did not appear.]
>
> In the circumstances of this case and bearing in mind the fact that the Court in assessing the reward for salvage takes into account not merely the actual expenses incurred but also the loss suffered by the salvor, I assess the reward of the salvor at Rs.20,000 and I also award him costs. After deducting Rs.1,000, the value of the launch handed over to the salvor's agent, the balance sum of Rs.19,000 and the cost should be paid out of the money deposited in Court.
>
> Judgement for Plaintiff

As far as I am concerned, the biggest mystery in this case is not where the opium came from, or what happened to the rest of the crew (if they died of hunger, how they must have wished that those tins really *did* hold condensed milk, instead of a fortune in narcotics!), but the customs valuation of the cargo. Who ever heard of *three quarters of a ton* of opium going for $6,000?

However, I digress. This judgment was encouraging to us because it showed that the Ceylon courts had ruled generously in rewards for salvage, and our operation, if it was to be counted as salvage, had certainly required far more skill than picking up a drifting motor launch.

But we hoped that we would not have to go to court to claim our reward. For we could not help noticing that it had taken Polish Ocean Lines of Gdyina four years to collect their money; we could not afford to wait that long.

[3] (1884) 9 P.D. 182, 186.

9

Celluloid Dreams

Throughout 1961, we quietly made plans and mapped out possible lines of action. One of our chief problems was security; it was impossible to keep the discovery completely secret, and the first leak had occurred at the lighthouse itself. Despite the precautions that Mike and the boys had taken, some of the staff had seen the coins, and rumors were soon rife. We were interested to hear, a few months later, that we had discovered a complete ship with all the standard trappings of gold bars and skeletons.

Since nobody could dive on the reef until the inter-monsoon calm nearly a year away, we had no immediate worries about claim jumpers. But it was obvious that we must waste no time when the new season began, and in order to operate efficiently we would have to have a boat— one that could carry divers and heavy equipment.

Such a vessel would cost a good deal of money, and I suggested that we hire one of the locally produced twenty-five-foot diesel-engined fishing boats which were steadily replacing the picturesque but inefficient traditional outriggers. It would not cost a great deal to modify it for our purposes; but Mike, who hates doing things in a small way, had more ambitious ideas. Nothing would satisfy him unless we had a boat all of our very own—a boat in which we could live and sleep and cook our meals, and be completely self-contained.

This, I calculated, would cost about $10,000, which was approximately ten times as much as we possessed between us, though it was rather less than what we owed. Where did we propose to get the money?

He had two answers. In the first place, he knew a shipyard where there was an unfinished twenty-eight-foot hull that would be just the thing for us; he could get it cheaply and pick up some secondhand engines, so it would not cost anything like $10,000. (If you know something about boats, you are doubtless already laughing.) And as for raising the money, he had an absolutely brilliant idea. He would make it in the local movie business.

I should explain that by this time Mike had completed only one film—the twenty-five-minute, sixteen millimeter Kodachrome short, *Beneath the Seas of Ceylon,* showing the adventures of Rodney with sharks and groupers on the Great Basses Reef. The projected *Boy Beneath the Sea* was still in the can (and still is, as I write these words two years later); despite its much greater potentialities and the unique footage of Mark and the three groupers, the events triggered by the discovery of the treasure had stopped it dead in its tracks.

Mike had learned a great deal about film making while editing and dubbing *Beneath the Seas of Ceylon*—but now he proposed to jump straight from that to a two-and-a-half-hour epic in Technicolor. *Two and a half hours?* you may well ask. Yes; that is the standard length for feature movies in the East. If they get less, audiences feel that they have been cheated. They also like lots of songs and dances, whether or not these have anything to do with the story.

Though the Ceylon film industry is quite active and has produced about seventy movies in Sinhalese, Mike's would be the first in color; if he could bring it off, this fact would obviously be a great asset. The film would also establish another first; we were quite sure that no other sunken treas-

CELLULOID DREAMS 63

ure film had ever been made with *genuine* sunken treasure.

This was a particularly delightful idea, because it would make the facts of the case so hopelessly confused. Once the news began to circulate that we were making a treasure film, everyone would assume that all the current rumors were typical film publicity. I even wondered if the reaction might go too far, so that we would never be able to convince anyone that our treasure was the real thing!

However, the whole idea of making such a film was obviously absurd. Though I had always maintained that Mike had the right temperament for a movie director (this was seldom intended as a compliment), it was ridiculous to imagine that we could produce a complete two-and-a-half hour Technicolor feature. I had been to Hollywood (and, although I did not know it, was shortly to go there again) and had seen the enormous resources required for even the most modest film.

But it was no good arguing with Mike, acutely conscious of Time's winged chariot hurrying near, and the fact that he was already two years older than the Orson Welles of *Citizen Kane.* He had made up his mind, and knew exactly what he wanted to do. Moreover, he had some training in movie making that many people would have envied.

A few years before, he had watched David Lean direct one of the great classics of the modern cinema, *The Bridge on the River Kwai.* (In fact, Mike appears in it for about two seconds; but so do most of the fair-skinned inhabitants of Ceylon.) And he had many friends in the movie business, notably the Irish producer William McQuitty, whose *Night to Remember*—a superbly re-created enactment of the *Titanic* tragedy—is one of the most ambitious movies made in Britain during recent years. The advice of all these friends, however, added up to that given by Sam Goldwyn many years ago: "In two words—Impossible!"

Mike went right ahead. First he persuaded the owner of one of the big Ceylon movie circuits to distribute the film when it was made; a glimpse into the treasure chest (which really has a most unsettling psychological effect even on hard-headed businessmen), helped to clinch this. Then he worked out a very involved deal that I never pretended to understand, but it went something like this: He borrowed enough money to shoot a few reels of film, then when this came back from Technicolor, he used it as security to borrow some *more* money—and so on in a kind of snowball or chain reaction. It was all rather hair-raising, and if anything went wrong anywhere along the line we'd be broke, with no assets but a few thousand feet of Eastmancolor Negative.

Soon Mike was dictating the script at the rate of thirty pages a day. I read it, and it sounded terrible. But then, so do all film scripts, with their stage directions, their camera angles and all the other technicalities. There is a long and involved process—indeed, a kind of magic—before words on paper can be transformed into dramatic or beautiful pictures on a screen; and Mike, as it turned out, had a natural understanding of that process.

The story was a complicated one involving a young man whose father, a diver, had been killed soon after bringing up some gold coins from a wreck. There were several juicy villains, some fine fights above and below water, a holy man who lived in a picturesque cave, a gruesome attempt to revive a corpse by magic—but let our old friend Synopsis tell the tale; I quote from the lavishly illustrated souvenir booklet we prepared for the World Premiere:

A rare golden coin puts our hero Bandu and his friends, Raju and Sena, on the track of a treasure galleon sunk off the island of Ranmuthu Duwa. They set out to recover it with diving equipment, but their plans are known to Dhanapala, a crafty jeweler, and Mutthusamy, a wealthy trader, who join forces against them. Meanwhile, Bandu has fallen in love with the beautiful

Kumari, Mutthusamy's daughter, who warns him of her father's plans.

A Sanyasi (holy man) tells the boys that, centuries ago, the local temple was looted and its treasure—including a great golden statue of the god—was carried off in a galleon. But a storm immediately destroyed the ship, and whoever touches the treasure with greed will be punished.

Dhanapala and Mutthusamy hire Renga, son of the local Kattadiya (soothsayer) Kalidas, to spy on the boys, who have now located the wreck. Renga steals their diving gear and finds the golden statue, but is drowned when his air hose is entangled in one of the deity's many arms. Thus the prophecy is fulfilled.

Kalidas, mad with grief, attempts to conjure up evil spirits to bring Renga back to life. Failing, he swears vengeance.

Meanwhile, Dhanapala summons an assassin, who sneaks up on Bandu while he is working on the wreck. In the resulting underwater fight, Bandu is victorious. A battle for the boat follows, in which Mutthusamy crosses to the boys' side and Dhanapala, entangled in the anchor rope, is dragged into the depths.

Kalidas, however, has kidnapped Kumari and chained her to the ancient rock of sacrifice at the mercy of the rising tide. The boys rescue her just as the water is about to cover her head. Finally, they restore the statue to the temple, and receive the holy man's blessing.

Yes, I know it sounds corny, and it is; but you might try squeezing *Hamlet* into as many words. *Ranmuthu Duwa*, incidentally, is Sinhalese for "Gold (and) Pearl Island,"— and was the title of the film. Remember that word *Ranmuthu* (pronounced Ran-mootoo); you will meet it again.

10

The Mysterious

Occident

At this point things began to move rather swiftly, in every direction except toward the Great Basses Reef. But all our activities, however variegated, were really aimed at that distant goal, which was never very far from our minds. I hope that I can impose some order on the chaos of this chapter—but if not, at least I trust that even its apparent irrelevancies are interesting.

Space, which I had somewhat neglected for the last few years (having thought of practically nothing else from 1935 to 1955) began once more to intrude itself into my life. Dr. Wernher von Braun, whom I had converted to skin diving during a weekend in Washington just before my departure to the Great Barrier Reef, wrote to ask if I would take charge of a panel discussion being arranged by the American Rocket Society in New York. I was able to say "Yes," thanks to those two admirable but somewhat dissimilar publications, *Reader's Digest* and *Playboy* magazine.

Reader's Digest, in a moment of wild abandon, had bought my novel *A Fall of Moondust* for its Condensed Book Club—

the first science-fiction ever to be inflicted upon its hapless membership. And *Playboy* had taken a large slab from my volume of scientific extrapolations *Profiles of the Future;* I am sorry about the commercials, but I would like to give credit where it is due, and without this timely aid we would have finished 1961 subsisting on boiled Eastmancolor.

Just before I left Ceylon at the beginning of August, I watched Mike shooting a scene with Mark Smith for *Boy Beneath the Sea,* and was depressed by the amount of time it took, and the multitude of lights, filters and general complication. Mike spent an entire evening getting three shots, and was still at it when I crept away after midnight, exhausted by the effort of watching. It was appalling to realize that there were more than a thousand separate shots in *Ranmuthu Duwa* (for comparison, there were only about seven hundred in *Bridge on the River Kwai*), and I began to wonder if we would live long enough to make the film, even if the money held out. But we were committed now; the contracts had been drawn up, the film stock had arrived—and the advances had been spent.

On my transit through London, I called at that archive of naval history, the National Maritime Museum, taking with me some photographs of the two small guns from the wreck. When these had been cleaned and the coral of two and a half centuries removed, we had found traces of milling and a pattern of engraved lines on one of the guns, and we had hoped that this would lead to their identification. But neither the National Maritime Museum, nor Mendel Peterson at the Smithsonian, had ever seen anything like this design; they could only guess that the guns were of Oriental workmanship. Even now we have not been able to discover anything about them; but they did their job when they led Mike and the boys to the wreck.

I also took with me a few of the Surat rupees, nicely cleaned and polished. Though I knew that single specimens were of no great value (the going rate is about a dollar, but of course we had no intention of unloading our thousands on the open market as ordinary coins, or of splitting the big lumps), I thought it would be interesting to sound out the experts. This led to a brief and unsatisfactory encounter with the small, weird world of the London antique business.

I called first at a very famous establishment in Mayfair; as soon as I stepped inside, I felt that I should really have used the tradesman's entrance. However, nervously fingering my tie (an article of clothing I had not worn for the past year), I inquired the way to the Coin Department, and presently found myself in a showroom that graciously combined the best attributes of country-house library and high-class funeral parlor.

An elegant young man glanced casually at my offering, and an expression of faint distaste flickered across his features.

"I'm afraid, sir," he said, in a voice that spoke of long experience with decayed nobility trying to dispose of family heirlooms, "that we wouldn't be interested."

Suitably crushed, I tried a different tack.

"What would you advise," I asked, "for anyone who had a large quantity—a *very* large quantity—of these coins for disposal?"

He looked thoughtfully at his fingernails. When he had counted them, and checked that they were all there, he conceded: "You *could* try an auction room."

"Such as?" I said, going for broke.

"I would recommend Messrs. Crypt, Cumberbund & Catafalque," he replied. "An excellent house—they can dispose of anything." (Sniff) "You'll find them at 6, Little Wimple Street."

I apologized for intruding, and left in search of Messrs. C. C. & C. Their establishment turned out to be a small shop, apparently uninhabited, and stuffed with antique sofas, chairs, harps, spinets and dim, gilt-framed paintings. There was an open door at the back, so I stuck my head through and called: "Is there anybody there?"

I *thought* I heard someone call, as from an immense distance "Please come in," so I started down a passageway which rapidly became more and more impenetrable. Contorted chairs, Victorian bric-a-brac, stuffed animals, music boxes, marble statues, complete sets of the *Encyclopaedia Britannica* for 1795, crowded in upon me until I could barely squeeze through. The air was so dusty, so redolent of the past, that I had difficulty in breathing. There was still no sign of life, and I began to feel like a refugee from an Alfred Hitchcock film. The urge to see once again the bright sunlight of Little Wimple Street while there was still time became quite overwhelming; my nerve broke, and I beat a cowardly retreat. I shall never know if I might have done business with Messrs. Crypt, Cumberland & Catafalque; but somehow I doubt it.

A few days later I was in the slightly different world of New York and, as usual, was immediately caught up in the hectic life of that stimulating and sleepless city. Indeed, no sooner had I checked into my New World base, the Hotel Chelsea on 23rd Street, when there was a long phone call from Hollywood and I was commanded to catch the next westbound jet.

This was all very well, but I'd arrived on a weekend and had only the clothes I was wearing; my spare suits were still in cold storage. So I felt a little scruffy when, a few hours later, I arrived at Los Angeles—and was deposited at the awe-inspiring Beverly Hills Hotel with one small hand case containing little more than toothbrush and electric shaver.

I hope that producers Dore Schary and Hubbell Robinson thought it was worthwhile; I certainly enjoyed talking to them for several hours at their expense (this will surprise numerous friends who would be prepared to contribute to a fund to insure my silence). A few weeks later I had the pleas-

ure of seeing, on TV, Tony Randall going through the rou-
tines I'd suggested; another bonus was being flown over the
Grand Canyon twice in twenty-four hours—for as soon as the
conference was over, I fled back to the less opulent standards
of the Hotel Chelsea; and to my spare suits.

When my psyche (then somewhere around the Azores)
had caught up with me again, I was ready for the next item
on my U.S. program—a conference of science-fiction writers
that takes place annually in the little town of Milford, Pennsylvania. I was collected at the Chelsea by Dr. John Pierce,
an old friend who has since acquired considerable fame,
thanks to a device called Telstar. For John is Director of
Communications Research of the Bell Laboratories, and was
directly responsible both for Echo, the giant balloon satellite,
and Telstar.

John drove me, in the smallest indigenous American car I
have ever seen (very handy for illegal U-turns), absent-
mindedly straight through the toll gate of the Pennsylvania
Turnpike and on to Milford. Here, among our fellow addicts,
we set up a bachelor establishment in a cottage on the banks
of the Delaware, and tried to avoid poisoning each other with
amateur cooking. This was my introduction to that brilliant
invention, the pre-packaged TV dinner; our icebox soon
looked like an aluminum mine.

It was here that I did my only skin diving in the United
States, among the exotic underwater fauna of the Delaware.
I was encouraged to do this by the example of another old
friend, Ted Thomas, who had brought his aqualung with him
and was determined to beat Washington by crossing the
Delaware *underneath*. (He did, too.)

Ted was another of my converts to skin diving—though he
goes in for a version that sets the goose pimples dancing on
my spine; he explores pot holes and flooded caves. He is welcome to them.

Ted, John and I shared a common interest not only in

science-fiction, but in communication satellites. As is now well known (and if not, it's neither my fault nor John Pierce's, who has acted as my unpaid publicity agent for many years), I was the first to lay down their fundamental principles in a technical paper published in *Wireless World* in 1945, and promoted them vigorously in my books through the early 'fifties. A few years ago Ted Thomas, who is a patent expert, spent some time looking into my legal rights in the matter. He made the interesting discoveries that (a) I couldn't have obtained a patent in 1945 as the idea was too far-fetched; (b) if I had, it would have expired the very year the first communication satellite was launched. So that was the end of my yacht.

The beginning of October saw me in Washington, for a slightly larger assembly than the Milford conference. This was the Twelfth Congress of the International Astronautical Federation, meeting for the first time in the United States. In 1951, when I had been Chairman of the Second Congress in London, I do not think that there were a hundred official delegates; now there were at least a thousand—including a strong contingent from the Soviet Union, headed by Professor Leonid Sedov.

The Washington visit gave me a chance of meeting Mendel Peterson at the Smithsonian, and seeing again the 1,000-rupee lump we had donated to the institution. And while I was in "Pete's" office, there was a long distance phone call from the most successful treasure hunter of modern times—Teddy Tucker in Bermuda. Teddy had found, amongst other items, several bars of gold and a magnificent jeweled bishop's cross, all of which he had later sold to the Bermuda government for $100,000. However, his negotiations with civil servants had not been easy, and at one stage in the proceedings he had reconsigned his treasure to the deep—until the government finally admitted that it belonged to him. I hoped that we would not have similar problems.

After this phone call, Pete and I invaded the impressive headquarters of the National Geographic Society—Pete carrying the twenty-five-pound lump of silver, I holding a fine Spanish rapier, encrusted with coral, which Tucker had just sent him. Thus armed, we had no difficulty in coercing the Geographic's officers to take us to lunch, and I was particularly pleased to meet Senior Editor Luis Marden, who discovered the wreck of the famous *Bounty* off Pitcairn. If I felt a little smug because our wreck was almost a century older than the *Bounty*, I had a surprise coming. For, in due course, Mike and I were to be joined by a diver with a wreck three *thousand* years older than ours.

Also in Washington, I was pleased to see Mark Smith once again—though I do not think that Mark was so pleased to be there, because he obviously missed Ceylon badly. Both he and Bobby Kriegel had returned to the United States, when their fathers' tours of duty in the East had finished. The boys will certainly never forget their days on the Great Basses Reef, and I am afraid that all the skin diving they do in the future will be something of an anticlimax. After all, you can hardly expect to stumble on a treasure ship twice in one lifetime.

The rest of my week in Washington was all concerned with space, though from time to time the Mogul rupees still jingling in my pocket did intrude into the conversation. Once, after Wernher von Braun told me that he was lecturing in Australia, we tried to work out schedules that would allow him to participate in our projected silver hunt. He was all for it, of course, but needless to say, it was one of those bright ideas that wouldn't work out. Probably, that was just as well; we would hate to have held up the Saturn program, and delayed the arrival of the first American on the moon.

One small incident at the Congress was to have a sequel in Ceylon, a few months later. I had just seen the film, *With Gagarin to the Stars,* and finding myself next to Professor

Sedov (then Chairman of the U.S.S.R. Commission on Astronautics), at dinner one evening, I could not resist launching a small space probe. "Why is it, Professor," I asked innocently, "that the rocket you see taking off at the end of Gagarin's film is only an intermediate range missile—not his vehicle at all?"

Professor Sedov is renowned for his deadpan sense of humor; when some U.S.A.F. guides once proudly showed him a towering Titan missile (height over a hundred feet), he is reputed to have asked: "What scale is this model?" So I was not surprised when he bounced straight back with "Well, from a distance all big rockets look the same."

The week in Washington was followed by an even more hectic one in New York. The American Rocket Society was having its Annual Meeting, and had combined this with a gigantic Space Flight Exposition at the Coliseum. The first three floors of this huge building were stuffed with more astronautical exhibits than had ever been shown to the public before—including the house-sized, million-and-a-half pound F.1. motor and the business end of Saturn, all large as life.

One of the planned highlights of this "Space Flight Report to the Nation" was the panel discussion that I had been asked to moderate. It was to evaluate the relative positions of the American and Russian space programs; the panel was perhaps one of the most distinguished ever assembled in this field, for it included Dr. von Braun, Dr. Hugh Dryden (Deputy Administrator of NASA), and General Bernard Schriever, head of the U.S. Air Force missile program. We had hoped to get Professor Sedov, but unfortunately the State Department had placed the Coliseum out of bounds.

Having seen many panel discussions fail to generate either light or heat because of excessively genteel chairmanship, I decided to be completely dictatorial and to ask all the questions myself. I had spent several weeks concocting these, which were designed to bring my panel nicely to the boil.

(For example, I asked General Schriever how we should set about integrating the U.S. and U.S.S.R. space programs.) The technique seemed to work well, and held an audience of almost three thousand for two hours; it was certainly a privilege to have been put in charge of so notable a team, and I am grateful for the good-natured way in which they responded to my needling.[1]

Now time was running out; the East was calling, more and more urgently, and I was anxious to see how Mike's movie making was progressing. The day before I flew out of New York I was amused to find an article in *Newsweek* entitled "Clarke of Ceylon." The title appealed to me; but whether Ceylon would be equally flattered was a different question.

---

[1] A full transcript of the panel will be found in the American Rocket Society's "Space Flight Report to the Nation."

11

Preparations

and Distractions

When I got back to Colombo, I was pleased (and surprised) to see how much progress had been made on the movie. Most of the exterior scenes had already been shot, around the great harbor of Trincomalee on the eastern side of the island. The scenery here is very picturesque and rugged; in sharp contrast to the flat, palm-fringed coast of the west, Trincomalee has rocky headlands and cliffs three or four hundred feet high. It was a perfect place for a movie villain to come to an end; so, needless to say, did one of ours.

I watched the filming as the life-sized dummy was pushed off the precipice; we only had the one dummy, and there could be no re-take once it had pitched into the boiling water three hundred feet below. It had to be right first time, and luckily it was; but when I calculated that this half-second shot had involved two days of work and a three-hundred-mile drive, I could hardly believe that the movie would ever be finished. As I have already remarked, it had more shots than *Bridge on the River Kwai;* and David Lean's budget had been approximately a thousand times as large as ours.

The film making at Trinco had not been without incident. One of the main props was an impressive, and indeed terrifying, statue of a multi-armed god, holding sundry swords, daggers, and skulls. This statue, which weighed about a quarter of a ton, had been sunk with great difficulty at the spot where Mike planned his underwater studio.

This was the deck, some twenty feet down, of what is probably the largest wreck in the world—an enormous, 40,000 ton floating dock, which was accidentally sunk during the war, while holding the battleship *Valiant*. When it had done its job, the statue was abandoned—and some months later the glittering, golden monster was discovered by the local fishermen. It caused great consternation, and nearly started a new religion, before the truth came out.

Curiously enough, when Mike was faking the recovery of the *genuine treasure,* he made an underwater discovery which may turn out to be of great archaeological importance. The scenes were being shot around the headland known as Swami Rock, which for at least two thousand years (some say three or four) has been the site of a famous Hindu shrine, the Konesar Temple.

In the seventeenth century, this great temple was destroyed and looted by the Portuguese, and the seabed at the foot of Swami Rock is littered with fallen columns, lintels, and blocks of stone jumbled together in hopeless confusion. Some years earlier, the priests of the present-day temple suggested to us that the ancient shrine's holy of holies, the sacred lingam (phallus) might be somewhere down there in the depths, but all the columns and pillars we had encountered had obviously been purely architectural, with alternating square and hexagonal sections.[1]

Yet one day, as he was hunting for locations in quite shallow water, Mike came across a perfectly cylindrical pillar—

[1] Our underwater exploration of the temple ruins and of the sunken dock, together with their histories, will be found in *The Reefs of Taprobane.*

the only one ever discovered on this submerged site. After great exertions, it was raised, carried a couple of hundred feet up the hill to the temple, and erected there at the auspicious moment decreed by the astrologers (of whom more anon). This event caused a considerable stir among the local Hindus, who regarded it as a fulfillment of an ancient prophecy, and a good omen for the future of the temple. We hoped that it was a good omen for the film and our projected expedition, now only three months in the future.

Our film-making activities had, of course, attracted a good deal of interest, and they had also done exactly what we had hoped, in diverting attention from the Great Basses Reef. Although we had now issued a guarded statement admitting that we *had* found sunken treasure, we had failed to specify where. The people who believed us thought it was off Trincomalee (and Rodney had generated additional confusion by vague hints about the Maldive Islands). The wise ones, of course, knew perfectly well that it was all a publicity stunt.

However, one bright journalist was convinced that something much more nefarious was afoot. I reproduce, in slightly shortened form, a "Letter to the Editor" which appeared in a small but incendiary local paper. Though it reduced us to hysterics at the time, it is really a rather sad example of the paranoic suspicions and raging inferiority complexes which all too often prevent East and West from meeting. Yet perhaps what annoyed Mike and me most was the fact that the writer did not even get our nationalities correct.

Sir,

It appears that a mound of Mogul era silver coins valued at Rs.10,000, found by Mr. Mike Wilson on the sea-bed off Trincomalee, is now on display at the Smithsonian Institute, Washington. The question arises as to who gifted or sold this treasure to the Smithsonian Institute even without giving a chance to the people of this country to view it in the local museums. Is it the Ameri-

cano (*sic*) Mr. Wilson or the spaceman Americano Mr.
Arthur Clarke and what right had they to do so? . . . All
the treasure recovered from the sunken ship belongs to
the government and people of this country because it
was found in Ceylon territorial waters. . . .

. . . In the past, the colonialists and their henchmen
plundered and carried away priceless art objects from
Asian lands to their own countries. Valuable treasures
from tombs of the Pharaohs, the Palaces of Sultans and
Maharajahs, taken by the shameless looters and their
intellectual brothers—the colonial archaeologists—now
repose in the British Museum, American Museums, and
in Museums all over Europe, lost forever to Asia and
Africa. . . . It is absolutely essential to find out whether
Messrs. Clarke and Wilson have smuggled out other
treasures too. Mr. Wilson is very fond of diving around
the Swami Rock on which stood the magnificent Hindu
Temple that was destroyed by the Portuguese vandals.
Suppose he finds some valuable objets d'art from the
bottom of the sea off the Rock, where will they end up?
In some American Museum?

Then followed several paragraphs suggesting that we were
importing color film into the country tax-free, evading Exchange Control regulations to pay for the processing, and
other pleasantries. The letter ended with this really superb
flight of imagination:

Foreign exchange is looming large in the operations of
Clarke Wilson Associates as well as other factors which
are much more important from a national point of view.
It is sufficient to state that before the liberation of Cuba,
hordes of American skin-divers explored the coasts of
Cuba and the Central Intelligence Agency had a detailed
map of Cuba's coastal defences. . . . Divers instructed by
the CIA helped to lay mines on Cuba's coasts to prevent

Castro's commandos from landing. What guarantee is there that the Central Intelligence Agency's agents have not dived around Ceylon's coasts and made comprehensive maps of coastal defences—especially of the Trincomalee harbour area—and scouted and marked suitable landing points for infiltrators and other forces.

. . . Considering all the diverse activities of these gentlemen leads one to the conclusions that there's really something fishy about the business of Arthur Clarke and Mike Wilson, under water and on land, among fishes and films, that needs a thorough investigation and remedial action.

Antiquarius

I have news for Antiquarius, whoever he may be. Mike's detailed plans of the Ceylon Navy's giant secret nuclear submarine base now repose safely in the Pentagon *and* the Kremlin. We believe in non-alignment.

And if anyone else is interested, our charges are very reasonable.

Back in Colombo, Mike took me to see the boat he had ordered. The twenty-eight-foot hull, very strongly built of timber that looked about two inches thick, was on the ways of a busy shipyard in the center of the city. I knew nothing at all about boats (today, I know more than I want to), but I was quite impressed and began to fancy myself at the wheel with a gold-braided yachting cap at a dashing angle.

There was one minor problem; as yet we had no engines. However, the boat did have a name, borrowed from the film: *Ran Muthu* ("Pearls and Gold"). By this time, it was not clear whether the movie was going to pay for the boat, or the boat for the movie. (It is still not at all clear, a couple of years later.)

Life was now quite complicated. Down at the shipyard, the hull of *Ran Muthu* was steadily taking shape. On the studio floor, so was *Ranmuthu Duwa*. But there were plenty of other distractions, such as the Underwater Murder Case. Actually, it was a briefcase; let me explain.

Though Mike gave up professional diving some years ago, odd jobs still occasionally come his way. He turns them down if he's busy, but accepts them if he's not, or if he's hard up. So usually he accepts them.

On this occasion, an insurance company had approached him, with the news that one of the government law officers had backed his car, at night, into a small lake. The legal gentleman had managed to get out before his Volkswagen sank (he was rather lucky), but he had lost all his papers in the car, and could Mike recover both?

So Mike put on his rubber suit, and plunged into the very muddy and insanitary lake. He found the car without any trouble, forced open the door, and emerged with a bulging briefcase, a thermos flask, and some sodden law books. On the next dive, to our great surprise, he managed to bring up the car. He correctly calculated that if he closed the windows and doors, and opened an aqualung cylinder inside the vehicle, the expanding air would blow out so much water that the car would float up to the surface. There was a great bubbling and seething, the beetle-like roof of the Volks emerged from the inky water, and Mike was able to push it to the bank.

It was then that we found why everyone was so anxious to recover the car and its contents. That briefcase held all the papers for the prosecution in a current murder trial. If we had known this interesting fact, we might have collected considerably more from the defense lawyers than from the insurance company.

The next distraction consisted of distinguished visitors. First were old friends who arrived quietly, without any publicity—Hans and Lotte Hass, whose adventures among sharks, sperm whales, and mantas have scared and inspired a whole generation of skin divers. We had met them last when their magnificent ship, the three-masted *Xarifa,* put into Colombo; but now, it seemed, they had given up underwater exploration. Hans had also given up his beard and looked fifteen years younger; Mike had acquired one, and looked ten years older. It was strange to show our films and treasure to the Hass's, whose exploits I had followed so avidly long before I had ever dreamed of diving myself.

The next visitor arrived aboard his own special four-engined jet, with all the publicity that press and radio could provide. He was then the most famous man in the world, and the first ever to escape from it; he was Yuri Gagarin.

Because all astronauts are interested in underwater exploration (though the reverse is not true), we had been asked to screen *Beneath the Seas of Ceylon* for the major; unfortunately, his hopelessly overcrowded program made this impossible. However, we were able to meet after a public lecture at which I threw him the question I had already tried on Professor Sedov: "Why doesn't your film show your rocket?" Needless to say, he evaded this diplomatically with "Well, when we can destroy all our war weapons, then we'll be able to show it."

I had a most curious impression of Gagarin as I watched him speak, up on the platform. Already he seemed remote from the human race, receding into history, and the words that Secretary of War Stanton is supposed to have spoken after the death of Lincoln came into my mind: "Now he belongs to the ages." Yet afterwards, chatting with him through the interpreter, he seemed a cheerful, friendly, and in no way unusual, young man, quite untouched by destiny. As some compensation for not being able to show him underwater Ceylon, I gave him this book's precursor, *Indian Ocean Adventure;* a few weeks later, I was pleased to receive his autobiography with the inscription: "To Arthur Clarke, this souvenir of our cosmic voyage and our meeting in Ceylon— Y. Gagarin."

It was now only three months before we were due to leave

on our expedition, and *Ran Muthu* still lacked engines. Then Mike made a disastrous bargain.

There is an area of Colombo known as Panchikawatte, which is one colossal junk yard. It consists of rows and rows of little sheds and shops, each surrounded by piles of rusting machinery, old tires, war surplus material, auto spares, and broken-down cars. Panchikawatte is a fascinating place to explore, because you never know what you'll find there. Even when you've bought it, you may still not know what it is.

Mike found a batch of 100 horsepower marine engines, complete with gear boxes, which had never been used. There was only one snag; they had been sitting in the junkyard since the end of World War II, and the Ceylon climate is not good for machinery. However, they started up when we tested them; so Mike beat the price down to just one third of that first asked, and carried off two units for $250 apiece. I suppose they cost the British Government, their original owners, at least five times this.

As he had no room for them at his house (which was now full of movie equipment, and film editors wrestling with miles and miles of *Ranmuthu Duwa*), he dumped them both on my doorstep. For the next few weeks, while the engines were being stripped down and cleaned, I had to step over crankshafts and pistons and starter motors and connecting rods each time I left the house. And every so often our quiet residential neighborhood would be shaken to its foundations by one of the engines starting up; it sounded like a Saturn rocket about to blast off, and made us rather unpopular.

Other bits and pieces for the expedition began to arrive. Perhaps the most essential item was an air compressor for our aqualungs, which have to be pumped up with air to a pressure of over a ton on every square inch. This requires a very special kind of compressor (about twenty times as powerful as the ones that garages use to pump up tires), and it had to be portable so that we could use it in out-of-the-way places, or even on the boat. A very neat and compact unit, the Cornelius 380, made by the Stewart-Warner Corporation, was flown out to us from the States; it could be easily carried by two men, yet would pump up an aqualung tank in only fifteen minutes.

Almost equally important were two "Redshank" rubber dinghies, very kindly given to us by the Avon Rubber Company. Though they folded up into a bag that could be easily stowed in the back of a car, the Redshanks could carry half a dozen men and several hundred pounds of equipment. You could fit an outboard motor on the back, and it was practically impossible to overturn them. They would be just the thing for shuttling between our boat and the reef.

To test the rubber dinghies, we took them down to the Colombo sea front. The city sprawls for about five miles along the coast of Ceylon, looking almost due west across the Indian Ocean to Africa. There is an interesting reef, with some coral and a fair selection of fish, only two hundred yards from the main road of the city. And I doubt if there is anywhere else in the world where you could see a whale, as I have done, spouting within a thousand feet of the House of Representatives. (Of course, I'm aware that whales have been known to spout *inside* such establishments.)

Floating over this reef in our rubber boat, and diving down to the weed-covered seabed only ten or fifteen feet below, we made a curious discovery. Every few yards we would come across little pits or craters in the rock, and at the bottom of these there would be dozens of lead musket balls, buried in sand. They had obviously been here for a couple of centuries, and there were so many in one area that we wondered if they had been accidentally dropped into the sea when a supply boat overturned. We had to give up this theory when we found how far and wide they were scattered; now we think that they may be the relics of a fierce battle fought in 1656 between the Portuguese defenders of Colombo and the invading Dutch. The siege lasted for months, and both sides must have shot off tremendous quantities of ammunition. But the problem of the musket balls is still unsettled; this is just another tantalizing fragment of underwater history—part of the great jigsaw that one could spend lifetimes trying to assemble.

However, according to certain experts, none of us had a lifetime ahead of him. For they believed—and so did thousands, if not millions, of people in the East—that the world was going to come to an end in one week's time.

12

The Stars

in Their Courses

On February 5, 1962, there would be a total eclipse of the sun. That is a common enough phenomenon; it occurs once or twice in every year. But this time something else would happen. All the planets visible to the naked eye— Mercury, Venus, Mars, Jupiter and Saturn—would be in a compact group close to the sun; and the astrologers were sure that this heralded disaster.

As a matter of fact, such close planetary groupings happen about once every century (the next will be on May 5, 2000, in case you're worried), and I wrote several articles for the local newspapers pointing this out. These helped to reassure some people, but not many. Even those who thought there was "nothing in it" felt it wise to take precautions; there were offerings and prayers all over Asia, and in the temples the monks were chanting night and day. Only a few national leaders, like Mr. Nehru, had the courage to stand up and say that these predictions were all nonsense.

February 5 dawned and went; absolutely nothing happened, except that some indignant clients assaulted the astrologers and demanded their money back. We continued to shoot the film and to get the boat ready for the expedition, now planned for next month.

Fatal February drew to a close; it had not brought the end of the world. But then, on its very last day, it nearly brought the end of me.

I was shopping in Colombo, buying equipment for the boat; most of our time now seemed to be spent buying equipment for the boat. Leaving one store, I misjudged the height of a doorway and crashed the top of my head against the lintel. It took me a few minutes to recover, and I had a painful scalp wound; but I felt none the worse. I got on my motor scooter, drove three miles home, played several vigorous games of table tennis, and ate a hearty dinner—my last for many months.

That night I became violently sick, and spent the next couple of days in bed. But, convinced that it was merely something I'd eaten (you get used to occasional stomach upsets in the East), I was not particularly worried, and never dreamed of calling in the doctor. By the time one did arrive on the scene, I was almost completely paralyzed and could barely breathe.

I have vague memories of being carried to hospital, where I was apparently delirious for several days. (The medical report uses the nasty word "manic," but at the time I thought I was perfectly rational.) A plaster collar fastened round my neck gave me the worst nights I have ever endured, for I was convinced that my spine was being slowly bent backwards until it was about to snap. In other interludes, I was dying of thirst while being buried in desiccated dust (I can still taste that dust). When I became aware of my surroundings again, I was approximately as strong as a two-hour-old kitten.

This is scarcely an exaggeration. Though I could just move one arm and one leg, I could do nothing with them. The greatest feat I could achieve, after long deliberation and careful planning, was a slow roll from my back on to one side. I can remember doing this in order to throw my weight on to the bell-push which summoned the nurse; the tubes of jelly that had once been my fingers were quite unable to overcome the spring that kept the switch from closing.

I think I must have missed an iron lung by the thickness of a nerve fiber. Although I could breathe without much trouble when perfectly relaxed, the slightest exertion left me gasping. I could not speak more than two or three words without panting for breath. Having my face washed was a frightful ordeal; I could barely endure the brief passage of the suffocating sponge over my nose.

After six weeks of being fed and bathed like a baby in a private hospital, I was carried home at just about the time we had planned to leave for the reef. The Great Basses wreck would be undisturbed for 1962, and it seemed most unlikely that it would ever be disturbed by me at any future date. Though I could sit up when propped in a chair, I was stuck there and had to ring a bell for help when I wanted to move. The doctors, who had diagnosed an unusual form of spinal injury, had promised that I would be able to walk again, though they warned me that my left arm would never be much good (it now looked as if it was constructed of matchsticks). Any more underwater activity was almost certainly out of the question.

Yet I was not too unhappy; I could read and write, and was in no discomfort. I was just incredibly weak—so weak that I had already forgotten what the fit human body could do, and sometimes found myself attempting movements which, after due reflection, I realized were impossible.

No one who has not been completely paralyzed can really appreciate the wonderful mechanism of the human body. My slow but steady recovery was like a new birth; for all its worries and unpleasantness, it was a voyage of discovery I am glad to have made. As the weeks went by, I reached and passed one milestone after another, recapitulating my infancy. There was the day when I could sit up in bed unaided; there was the day when I could reach the bathroom by myself; there was the day (a good deal later) when I could *leave* the bathroom by myself; there was the day when I could rise from a chair using both arms, then one arm, then *no* arms. And finally I was able to walk, with the aid of two sticks, for as much as a dozen yards.

During this period I received one major psychological boost which contributed a good deal to my recovery. This was the news from UNESCO that I had been awarded the 1961 Kalinga Prize for the popularization of science. It was the tenth of these annual £1,000 awards (personal donations of the Indian industrialist and statesman, Mr. B. Patnaik, of whom you will be hearing a great deal in the years after Nehru), and the earlier winners included Bertrand Russell, Sir Julian Huxley, George Gamow, and Prince Louis de Broglie.[1]

With this stimulus, I felt the creative urge again, and began working on a boy's book called *Dolphin Island.* I wrote a couple of pages every day in pencil, while propped up in my chair—and got my secretary to type them out while I could still remember what the squiggles meant. *Dolphin Island* went very smoothly, being completed in six weeks, but when it was finished I felt rather sad. I could not help thinking that it was probably my farewell to the sea, which had given me so many strange, wonderful, and exciting experiences.

Then all else was banished by the arrival of Mike's movie, which we had been awaiting with growing impatience and anxiety for weeks. We rushed the seventeen large cans of film round to a local cinema, and two and a half hours later emerged feeling on top of the world. There was no doubt

[1] The 1962 award has gone to Gerard Piel, publisher of *Scientific American.*

that Mike and his little team of co-workers had made a winner. There were a few rough patches, but on the whole *Ranmuthu Duwa* was completely professional—and the color was lovely. I have never grown tired of watching the scenes of dawn over the great temples, the sea-washed cliffs of Trincomalee, the lines of pilgrims descending the sacred mountain known as Adam's Peak, and the mysterious underwater sequences—many of them shot on the Great Basses. For a first attempt at professional movie making, it was an astonishing effort.

RMD (as we now called it) turned out to be a smash hit, and its catchy songs were soon blaring out of every radio. Within a few months it had been seen by a million people—a tenth of the population of the country—and had created a great reservoir of good will for us. Wherever we went, the members of our diving team who had played parts in the movie were recognized and cheered (if they were Good Guys) or hissed (if they weren't).

I was now just strong enough to totter up the gangway of a Comet, so flew back to England to prove to my friends and family that I was still alive—as well as to see if there was any medical treatment available there which I could not get in Ceylon. There wasn't; but the British specialists confused the issue thoroughly by maintaining that my trouble was polio—whereas in Colombo I had been assured that it was a bang on the head that had laid me low. There is not much that a mere patient can do when the experts disagree; I would have preferred polio, which was likely to gain me more sympathy than my own carelessness. However, a few months earlier the famous racing motorist Stirling Moss had produced almost exactly the same symptoms as mine by crashing at 150 m.p.h. If the Colombo specialists were right—as they still insist that they were—I could at least claim to have done a somewhat more thorough job under my own power.

Six quiet weeks in England did me a lot of good; at least I

arrived using two sticks and left with only one, when I flew to New Delhi at the end of September to receive the Kalinga Prize. It was my first visit to India, though I had lived next door for five years. Unfortunately, I was not able to see much of this enormous country during my brief visit, for even one morning's sightseeing in Old Delhi left me totally exhausted. However, I held together long enough to meet the Director-General of UNESCO, M. Rene Maheu, and Mr. Patnaik, the donor of the prize, as well as numerous officials, scientists, and politicians. Then, back to Ceylon—and to my first trip in the good ship *Ran Muthu*.

A great deal had happened to her in the past few months. The war-surplus marine engines that Mike had bought so cheaply had been duly installed—and a horrid sight they looked, with their tangles of ignition cables, fuel lines, and cooling pipes. What made me still more unhappy were the fifty-gallon gas tanks; they would cost about a hundred dollars a time to fill, and the engines wouldn't take long to gulp them dry. And if the gas leaked, in these tropical temperatures, we would be sitting on top of an unexploded bomb.

It was a great relief when Mike decided to forget the whole idea, and switched to a pair of brand new diesels—far simpler, safer and more economical than the gasoline engines, though, of course, they made our original cost estimates look even sillier than they already were. (I had begun to feel that we were running a space program.) These engines took us, one calm, bright Sunday, chugging gently round the vast expanses of Colombo's port, which is one of the biggest artificial harbors in the world. We anchored for tea in the shadows of great ocean liners that weighed approximately ten thousand times as much as our boat, and watched the chart of the echo-sounder trace the contours of the seabed. *Ran Muthu* felt very solid and stable, and I was sure that she would do the job for which we had destined her.

I was less happy about Mike's other marine activities. Possibly because *Ran Muthu* would only do ten knots flat out, he had felt an urgent need for something faster, and had started to build a hydroplane. This diabolical device looked rather like an ironing board with Mike at one end and an outboard motor at the other, and was supposed to do about sixty miles an hour. He had called it *Psycho,* as a tribute to our mutual acquaintance, Robert Bloch, who has, I suppose, now scared more people out of their wits than anyone since Mary Wollstonecraft Shelley.

Psycho also scared quite a few people—including Mike. I saw its debut at a speedboat race on a large lake a few miles from Colombo; we had a grandstand view from an island packed with hundreds of sightseers who had come across by ferry. On the first turn around the course, *Psycho* bucked and threw Mike into the water; then, unhampered by the weight of a pilot, it started charging across the lake like a rocket. It took a great sweep round the island—and then, with uncanny accuracy, roared straight at the (luckily empty) ferry boat, tearing a hole in its hull a yard wide. *Psycho* itself was almost undamaged, and Mike tried his luck again in a later event with happier results—but the ferry was put completely out of action. We were able to escape from the island in a small boat of our own, but how the hundreds of spectators got off before cannibalism set in, if indeed they did, is something I shall never know.

I started this chapter with soothsayers; I have to end it with them. One night, during a violent storm, our Volkswagen van was stolen from outside Mike's house. This was a serious blow, because no new motor vehicles were being imported into the country and it was worth about $5,000—twice its insured value. The police were unable to find any clues, so supernatural aid was invoked.

It was some time before I realized what was happening; my views on the subject being well known, I was kept carefully out of the picture. But presently I became aware that members of our film unit were shooting off to odd parts of the island, and returning a day or two later with somewhat shamefaced expressions. Various clairvoyants had given them "infallible" leads; but every one of them, alas, appeared to have his crystal ball out of focus. As I was anxious to get the van back, I would have been happy to have my scepticism refuted.

Instead, it was only confirmed. The Volkswagen turned up a month later, on the other side of the island—and quite unrecognizable. It had been repainted, the engine had been changed, and the body had been carefully disguised as that of an earlier model. We would never have found it if there had not been a falling out among the thieves.

And all the soothsayers had missed the target completely. I don't think any of them had been within fifty miles of the van—and Ceylon is only a hundred and fifty miles wide. I could have done better with a pin.

13

False Start

When 1963 dawned, and the launching time for the next expedition was less than four months away, I had no idea whether I would be able to go with it. I could now walk steadily, though slowly, and was swimming every day, even more slowly. My left arm was obviously never going to be much good, but it was no longer completely useless and could even provide a measurable amount of thrust. (The first time I had tried to swim the crawl, I had merely revolved in counter-clockwise circles.)

Perhaps most encouraging of all, I could use an aqualung without difficulty. Nine months ago I had been scarcely able to breathe on land; now I could breathe comfortably underwater. This was certainly a great improvement.

So while Mike worked on *Ran Muthu* (not to mention *Psycho* and its still more high spirited successor *Pegasus*), I exercised and trained and struggled to lift minute weights with my moribund left triceps. By the beginning of March— exactly a year after the accident—I had made up my mind that I *would* go to the Great Basses. I did not expect that I would be able to dive, but I was sure that I could watch operations without getting in the way.

The plan of campaign was as follows. As soon as the

93

weather looked promising, Mike and Rodney, with our two boatmen Martin and Laza, would sail *Ran Muthu* out of Colombo harbor and head down the coast. They would aim for the nearest sheltered anchorage to the reef—the small fishing town of Tangalle. (See p. xviii.) Meanwhile, the rest of us would follow by land with the cameras, air compressor, and the delicate equipment we did not want to send by sea. When we had made our rendezvous, and if conditions further along this exposed coast seemed satisfactory, we would move on to Kirinda and begin operations.

Ran Muthu left Colombo on March 16, 1963, and she barely made it. The 16th was a Saturday, and the lock gates through which she would have to pass shut at noon for the weekend. We spent the entire morning, from 5 A.M. onwards, in one frantic rush, trying to get hold of essential items that had been forgotten until the last moment. But when I arrived at the shipyard at 10 A.M., I was astonished to see how neatly Mike had stowed away a small mountain of equipment aboard the boat, tucking it into her numerous lockers and cupboards.

I was promptly dispatched on a last minute round of shopping for such typically varied items as fifty fathoms of nylon rope (to which, at a later date, I was to entrust my life), a set of watchmaker's tools, a hacksaw, and a bicycle pump for pressurizing underwater camera cases. These I was able to round up on a quick tour of Colombo's shopping center aboard my Vespa. Though the doctors took a poor view of it, I found that I could now ride a scooter with complete confidence, and it was splendid for my morale to be able to move around without relying upon anyone else.

On this last-minute purchasing mission, I had a slight shock. As I placed my order in one hardware store, the manager commented, "So you're off to Kirinda?" I felt rather as General Eisenhower would have if, on June 5, 1944, a stranger in a London street has casually remarked: "So you're

invading Europe tomorrow?" Well, security hardly mattered
now; we were on our way—I hoped.

Ran Muthu had about ten minutes to spare when she
chugged away from the boatyard on Beira Lake, in the very
heart of the city, at which she had been built. To get from the
lake to the harbor she had first to go through a lock where
the water level dropped about ten feet, then pass through a
large tunnel that ran under some of the main roads of the
city. So part of *Ran Muthu*'s journey out to sea was by
subway.

By jumping on my motor scooter, I was able to catch the
boat at strategic points and take photos of the voyagers as
they left on their adventure. *Ran Muthu* looked incredibly
tiny as she sailed through the harbor, past the ocean liners
and freighters that visit Colombo from almost every port in
the world. I caught my last glimpse of her as she was passing
the lighthouse at the end of the enormous sea wall that
guards the harbor from the monsoon gales. Mike had a tape
recorder on board, with several spools of music, and as *Ran
Muthu* headed south down the coast I could hear faintly,
drifting across the Indian Ocean, "The Ride of the Valkyrie,"
Then I went home, started on my own packing, and waited
for news of the expedition.

When it came the next evening, it wasn't good—but it
might have been worse. At least *Ran Muthu* had reached
Tangalle—just. Mike phoned to say that he had crept into
harbor on half an engine, as *both* pumps in the water cooling
systems had broken down. He also reported that the weather
was rough, so there was no point in pressing on to Kirinda
even if he could.

I arranged for a mechanic and spare water pumps to be
rushed down by train and bus, and prepared to follow in a
rather beat-up Oxford van. (Our Volkswagen, a much more
suitable vehicle, was still in the hands of the police as Exhibit A.) Loaded with aqualung cylinders and other equip-

ment, the Oxford had a top speed of about forty m.p.h., but it got us safely to Tangalle. I did not drive; I have never done so since the day I took my driving test in Sydney in 1955. Though I managed to convince the examiner that I should have a license, I did not convince myself, and have been waiting ever since for fully automatic steering. On this trip, I lay back and admired the scenery while all the work was done by my companion, Hector Ekanayake.

Hector is a useful person to have on any expedition; apart from being a competent diver and photographer, he was the youngest boxer ever to become flyweight champion of Ceylon, and is now, on the strength of his first film appearance, one of the best-known people in the island. As the young thug Renga, he had two big scenes in *Ranmuthu Duwa;* one was a really magnificent free-for-all with the hero, which Hector made most convincing as he knew how to pull punches. (The hero didn't, but Hector could absorb them.) The second scene was even more memorable, though it required little acting talent, for in it Renga was a singularly gruesome corpse. He was laid out in a cave beside a small spring which bubbled blood from time to time, while his distraught father tried, with disastrous results, to conjure up a demon who would restore him to life. All this made a great hit with the public, and nowadays Hector cannot go anywhere without collecting crowds and cries of "Renga!" Though he pretends otherwise, he really enjoys this; but I fear he has become irrevocably type-cast.

When we arrived at Tangalle, we found *Ran Muthu* anchored in the little bay just in front of the resthouse, which Mike had more or less taken over as the expedition's temporary base. A resthouse is Ceylon's nearest equivalent to a motel; a few are excellent, but many have gone steadily downhill since they were built by the Dutch a couple of centuries ago. At Tangalle, we were driven out of the best room by bugs, and retreated in good order behind a barrage of

DDT. But we were well fed by a friendly staff, and Tangalle is such a beautiful place that I would be content to stay there indefinitely.

To the east of the resthouse there is a tremendous sweep of palm-fringed bay, providing a safe anchorage for dozens of fishing boats. To the west, the view is quite different; there is a small headland above the town, and when you have climbed that you can see along the coast for mile after mile, past a whole series of out-thrust capes, each one becoming bluer and more mysterious with distance.

Not long ago I reread an article called "In Search of Paradise" by Santha Rama Rau (*Horizon*, March 1961). Here the much-traveled Miss Rau discussed Bali, Kashmir, Capri, and other real-life approximations to Shangri-La; and after considering them all she decided that the nearest to a genuine paradise is "the south coast of the island of Ceylon, scalloped with perfect beaches, fringed with coconut palms, and beyond, the emerald sea stretching all the way to Antarctica." That is a good description of Tangalle, and I am prepared to add my vote to Miss Rau's.

But paradise had its problems, as well as its bedbugs. Though *Ran Muthu's* water pumps had been fixed (the trouble was faulty lubrication—we had been recommended the wrong grease), the sea was choppy and there was a gusty wind. Until the weather was calmer, it was pointless—if not dangerous—to move to Kirinda. However, we could do some background filming while we were stuck at Tangalle, so on the day after my arrival *Ran Muthu* pulled up her anchor and chugged out into the middle of the bay, taking divers and slightly seasick cameramen.

I remained on land, photographing her departure—and watching a humpback whale which came into the bay during the morning. Perhaps the sight of this seagoing mammal lured me into the water, for I decided to go snorkeling just off shore. Although visibility was not very good (in Ceylon, this means less than twenty feet), it was delightful to be swimming over coral again, for the first time in two years, and to meet old friends like Surgeon fish, Angels, and Korans. This was only a dozen yards from the resthouse; one could practically walk off the veranda and straight into the sea.

When *Ran Muthu* arrived back at lunchtime after her brief excursion out into the bay, Mike had some hair-raising news. Unknown to all of us until that morning, the expedition had been literally within a few thousandths of an inch of complete disaster. And when I say "literally," I *mean* literally —and not, like so many writers these days, metaphorically. Another thousandth of an inch, and the boat and everyone aboard her might have been blown skyhigh. What I shall describe is, as far as I know, unique—but it could happen very easily to any divers, and the next paragraph may save some reader's life.

I mentioned that everything had been stowed away very neatly in the lockers and cubbyholes of the boat. This included half a dozen aqualung cylinders, fully charged to their working pressure of 2,200 pounds to the square inch. That was safe enough; but no one had realized that two tanks had been tucked under the battery compartment—and ever since *Ran Muthu* had left Colombo, acid had been slowly dripping on to high-tensile steel cylinders stressed to a total internal pressure of about a thousand tons. When we discovered this, the metal was already deeply etched; we did not breathe again until we had opened the valves and the last of the air had hissed angrily away. (Yes, this would be a good way to make a time bomb; I pass the idea on to anyone who may be professionally interested.)

After lunch, the weather had improved somewhat and Mike decided to push on with the boat; I would remain at the resthouse with Hector and our photographer until Mike phoned back to say that he'd arrived safely. Next morning, he called me from Hambantota—about halfway between

Tangalle and the reef—with the news that conditions had turned poor again and that he was heading back. I was not surprised, for the wind was now blowing heavily and spray was drifting off the breakers like clouds of smoke.

So we waited, scanning the horizon for the first sight of the returning boat. I had brought with me, for just such a purpose, the finest small telescope ever built—the 3½-inch Questar, a jewel of precision optics which has produced close-ups of the moon that could easily be mistaken for Mount Wilson photographs. Although the barrel is only eight inches long (this book would hide it completely), a combination of lens and mirror makes the light traverse the tube three times, with the result that the instrument is equivalent to one a yard in length. Various eyepieces give magnifications of up to 180, though it is easy to go higher than this on those rare occasions when the clarity of the atmosphere permits. There is an electric drive in the base that will keep the field of view centered on a star all night— no, I am not getting a penny from the Questar Corporation, but perhaps I had better stop here.

In the middle of the morning, as I scanned the horizon, I caught my first glimpse of *Ran Muthu's* canvas hood, bobbing intermittently above the edge of the earth. As she crawled over the skyline, she looked like a jeep just awash; it was more than an hour before she reached us and dropped anchor outside the resthouse. The telescope had saved us a great deal of anxiety and worry, and it was to save me a good deal more in the weeks to come.

While we were waiting for the boat to arrive, a group of the local fishermen brought in their catch—including a shark about eight feet long. I took some photographs while Hector examined it thoughtfully and reconsidered his enthusiasm for diving. A dead shark is a hideous and sinister object; no one, seeing it stranded out of its natural element, could ever imagine its beauty and grace as it sweeps over the seabed. I suspect that a man will look even uglier when exposed to the vacuum of space; we shall soon know.

It was a waste of time and money for the whole team to wait at Tangalle while the weather improved, and Mike had two urgent reasons for returning to Colombo. A few years earlier he had married Elizabeth Perera, one of the most beautiful girls in Ceylon (which is saying a good deal) and she was about to found the Wilson dynasty. For the last few days Mike had been going around with a distracted look, but this was not altogether due to incipient fatherhood. The local powerboat enthusiasts were arranging a meet, and he was afraid he would miss it through (a) Elizabeth or (b) the Great Basses Reef. He was only too happy, therefore, to leave *Ran Muthu* at Tangalle and to hurry back to Colombo.

Though the baby's arrival was imminent, it was not—unlike the boatrace—definitely scheduled. Mike had a choice between hovering around the nursing home, and heading out of town with his hydroplane *Pegasus*. He left town.

The first race was starting, in a large river estuary twenty miles south of Colombo, when the public address system announced that competitor Mike Wilson had just been presented with a daughter. He promptly boarded *Pegasus*, and took it skimming round the course at sixty miles an hour. Even so, he did not forget his gamesmanship in his exuberance; the other entrants did not realize that he still had ten miles an hour up his sleeve. By the time the day was over, he had won everything in sight.

I was the first to arrive back at the hospital, where I found Elizabeth looking perfectly normal and composed, just as if she had come straight from a fashion parade. Only the presence of a six-pound bundle in the corner revealed that anything out of the way had happened. When Mike turned up, a little later, he was so festooned with silver cups and shields that he clanked like one of the Knights of the Round Table; if baby Anne's consciousness registered the arrival of her father, it must have been a traumatic experience.

From the expedition's point of view, Anne could not have chosen a more awkward time to make her appearance. Owing to the incompatibility of her parents' blood groupings, she needed an immediate transfusion and had to remain in hospital, so Mike could not possibly leave Colombo until she was out of danger. And it was at this very moment that we received news that our rivals—the divers who had killed our tame groupers—were on the way back to the reef.

We had done our best, of course, to disguise our objective, but it is hard to keep a secret in Ceylon and by this time anyone who was interested must have had a very good idea just why *Ran Muthu* was hanging around the south coast; I have already mentioned my shock in the hardware store. We could scarcely blame poor little Anne for keeping us all biting our fingernails in Colombo, but we could see a fortune slipping from our grasp while we waited for the doctors to give the all-clear. It was a most nerve-wracking and frustrating situation, and a melodramatically improbable one. Who had ever heard of treasure hunters held up by a baby, while their rivals raced to the scene?

We were quite sure that no other divers would be able to find the site in a hurry, even if they had an approximate idea of its location. But the danger was there, so we had to do something to safeguard our interests, and to protect all the money and effort we had invested in the expedition.

Apart from direct action with dynamite and gasoline (both popular with local fishermen wishing to inconvenience their competitors), our only defense was a rather frail one provided by the law. For in our researches, we had now discovered something about the wreck which appeared to change its entire status.

In Chapter 8, I mentioned that it was just outside the limit of six nautical miles (almost seven statute miles) claimed by Ceylon as its territorial waters. This seemed to place it in the open sea, where it was fair game for anyone who could get there first. However, during the last few weeks we had discovered a Ceylon government order dated August 3, 1891, which cast a new light on the subject.

We, Sir Arthur Elibank Havelock, Knight Commander of the Most Distinguished Order of Saint Michael and Saint George, Governor and Commander-in-Chief in and over the Island of Ceylon and its dependencies, in pursuance of Her Majesty's Command [did declare that] from and after the declaration of these Our Letters Patent in our Island of Ceylon, the said Great Basses Rock and Little Basses Rock shall be annexed to, and become Dependencies of, our said Island of Ceylon, and shall be subject to the law from time to time in force in Our Island. . . .

Here was the sort of problem on which international lawyers thrive. Though our wreck was outside the six mile limit *from the mainland,* it was less than half a mile from the Great Basses Rock, and that was now regarded as part of Ceylon. If it was legitimate to draw a six-mile circle around the Great Basses Rock, then our wreck would be within the jurisdiction of Ceylon!

Homi Rustomjee dived into his law books again, and came up with the following memorandum:

The question as to the extent of the territorial waters of Ceylon has to be determined. The practice of International Law is to recognise that a State's territorial waters extend up to three nautical miles from its shores.

By a Proclamation dated 20th December 1957 the territorial waters of Ceylon have been declared to extend to a distance of six nautical miles from the appropriate base line.

In a work called *The Law and Custom of the Sea* by H. A. Smith, Professor Emeritus of International Law in the University of London, the learned author states on page 6: "Territorial waters extend seawards from their base line to a width of three nautical miles. Some states make more extensive claims, but none claim less, and there is a preponderance of opinion among the chief maritime powers, including Great Britain, that claims to a wider belt than three miles cannot be accepted.

Finally, by an Order in Council issued in the reign of Her Majesty Queen Victoria the territory known as "Great Basses" and "Little Basses" has been annexed and declared to belong to the Island of Ceylon. The question immediately arises as to whether the extent of Ceylon's territorial waters has been affected by such annexation. In the work referred to above, the learned author states on page 7: "If the coast line is fairly regular, in the sense that it is neither deeply indented nor fringed with islands, there is general agreement that the territorial belt must be measured from the low water mark of spring tides."

Again in the section dealing with "The Base Line of Territorial Waters" on page 10, he says, "Questions have sometimes been raised about such points as lighthouses, uninhabited rocks, sandbanks, etc. Insofar as British Courts are concerned, the question was really settled by a prize decision of Lord Stowell in 1805, when he held that a mud flat near the mouth of the Mississippi carried with it its own belt of territorial waters, and this point of view has subsequently been maintained by the Foreign Office in various diplomatic exchanges. In principle Lord Stowell's decision, which has recently been followed in the United States, seems to be clearly right. Any such piece of land is either a part of the national territory or it is not. If it is part of the territory, there seems to be no reason why the ordinary rule should not apply. The question whether or not it is habitable or used in any way is quite irrelevant. If it is not part of the territory of any state, then it is clearly a *res nullius,* a "no-man's land," and as such open to occupation or annexation by the first comer.

It is clear therefore that the question whether any wreck found in the areas of the "Great Basses" and the "Little Basses" have to be delivered to a Receiver of Wrecks will have to be considered in the light of the above referred to Order in Council. It will have to be decided whether such Order in Council has in any manner affected what is regarded as the belt of territorial waters of Ceylon and the normally accepted or recognized manner of computing the extent of such belt.

There thus seemed at least a *prima facie* case for considering that our wreck lay in Ceylon waters, though the final decision would rest with the government's law officers— probably the attorney general. It would certainly take many months to decide this, but meanwhile we could use the situation to our advantage. We had kept the very helpful archaeological commissioner, Dr. C. E. Godakumbure, fully informed of our plans, and we requested him to issue us a permit to excavate the wreck site, under the usual terms granted to workers wishing to make a "dig" in Ceylon. With this piece of paper in our hands, we were the only group (we hoped) legally authorized to "excavate for antiquities" on the Great Basses.

Using this permit like a talisman, we contacted the police on the coastline along the reef, asking them to watch out for anyone disturbing the site; we also alerted the lighthouse authorities, because the men in the tower would have a grandstand view of any activities in the area. Not that they could do much to stop it, but at least they could send a warning to shore, when they flashed their nightly report by Morse signal lamp.

After that, there was nothing that we could do but to sit

and keep our fingers crossed, and to wait until baby Anne changed from her present shade of yellow to a healthy pink. However, it is an ill wind that blows no good; our enforced stay in Colombo brought us one tremendous piece of luck which altered the whole character of our expedition. It arrived, on the auspicious date of April 1, in a letter festooned with strange stamps and bearing the postmark Athens, Greece.

14

Kirinda Beach

The letter was from one Peter Throckmorton, saying that he'd been working on numerous wrecks of archaeological importance in the Mediterranean and Aegean, and perhaps we would let him know if there was anything interesting around Ceylon.

Mike and I looked at each other. Was there, indeed? Then the writer's name rang a bell, and when I ran through my *National Geographic* files I soon discovered why. Peter Throckmorton had been responsible for the discovery and subsequent excavation, with a team from the University of Pennsylvania, of the oldest wreck ever found—a 1,300 B.C. Bronze Age trader that had gone down at Gelidonya, off the coast of Turkey.

As we read Peter Throckmorton's articles,[1] and studied the techniques used to investigate this incredibly ancient wreck, we knew at once that we needed his experience very badly on our own expedition. But we hoped to leave again in two or three days, and we were not even sure if he was in Athens, still less what his timetable was.

After much argument, which as usual Mike won, we took

[1] See "Thirty-three Centuries Under the Sea" (*National Geographic,* May 1960) and "Oldest Known Shipwreck Yields Bronze Age Cargo" (*Ibid.,* May 1962).

a chance and cabled: CAN YOU COME AT ONCE IF WE SEND RE-
TURN AIR TICKET? CAN PROMISE INTERESTING WRECK. I might
add that at the time we didn't have the money for the ticket,
but I possess that useful invention the Air Credit Card, which
enables you to fly now and face the consequences later.

While we waited to hear from Peter Throckmorton, and
Mike hovered round the nursing home keeping an eye on the
baby's progress, I decided to take a quick run down the coast
to check on conditions at Tangalle and Kirinda—and to see
if there was any sign of our rivals. There had also been a
small mutiny aboard *Ran Muthu,* still at anchor in front of
the resthouse, and it appeared necessary to bang a few heads
together. Hector would be very glad to do this, but I was
annoyed that the necessity had arisen, when we had so
many other things to worry about.

However, on the drive down the coast I saw something
that took a great weight off my mind. It was the boat which,
rumor had it, was taking our rivals to the Great Basses—but
it was in such a battered and decrepit condition that I very
much doubted if it would get there. And if it did, it would
probably stay. I decided there and then that our worries had
been groundless, though it would not be wise to write off the
opposition completely.

When we arrived at Tangalle, we met Rodney, who told
us that conditions along the coast had been excellent for the
last few days. So when order had been restored aboard *Ran
Muthu,* we drove on to Kirinda, and I had my first glimpse
of the Great Basses Reef in four years.

At the lighthouse station, the sea was fairly calm, with
small breakers making half-hearted assaults on the beach
from time to time. But what was it like out there at the
lighthouse, just visible as a tiny mark on the horizon?

A small hill, or rather a giant rock, looms above the village
of Kirinda, and from its summit one can get a marvelous view
of the surrounding landscape. On the top of the hill is an

attractive little Buddhist shrine, and we climbed up to this, carrying Questar and tripod. After paying our respects to the *bikkhu* (monk), we set up the telescope and I gazed out to sea.

There was the lighthouse, poised on the very rim of the world. In this tropical heat, with the sun burning down from overhead, the atmosphere danced and trembled, and the image was never still for an instant. But as I stared through the eyepiece, and waited for the fleeting moments when the picture steadied itself, I could pick out a whole host of familiar details, on that rock ten miles away in the Indian Ocean.

I could see the crane that had hauled us and our gear from the relief boat, four years ago. There were men moving around on the lower platform; had the atmosphere been steady enough for me to use the full power of the telescope, I might have been able to recognize them. The weathervane and the great lamp house were easily visible; I could even catch occasional glimpses of the massive diamond-shaped panes of glass which protected the light. Oddest of all, from my viewpoint, two of the tower's deeply recessed windows were exactly in line, so I could look straight through the middle of the lighthouse into a patch of blue sky.

But the reef was what really interested me. I scanned the telescope along the horizon—and there it was. Unmistakable on the skyline was the dark triangle I had christened Shark's Tooth Rock. The highest part of the reef, it must have claimed many ships over the centuries; to us, it was useful as a landmark. By taking a sight on it, Mike could locate the wreck with complete accuracy, in the classic pirate-treasure tradition.

Around Shark's Tooth Rock, the sea was never still. But it was breaking lazily, without violence. Most of the time, the rock was completely exposed; only once in every few minutes did the swell surge over it, or a curtain of spray hide it momentarily from view. As far as I could judge, it would be safe to dive there.

Like Moses looking into the Promised Land, I stared at that remote and tantalizing patch of sea, foaming whitely on the horizon. After all the difficulties and disappointments we had already endured, would we *ever* get there? And would it be worth the trouble—or had Mike and the boys found everything that mattered?

In a few days, we should know the answers.

When I got back to Colombo to report that all was well, Mike had good news for me. Peter Throckmorton had cabled to say that he could come, so I dusted the cobwebs off my Air Travel Card and booked his ticket. He arrived four days later, loaded with specialized underwater equipment—such as a pair of Captain Cousteau's neat little Calypso cameras, which work above or below water with equal ease, and a submarine balloon for hoisting heavy objects from the sea-bed. He also brought with him a fascinating collection of color slides of his 3,200 year old Bronze Age cargo ship, and gave us an illustrated lecture that very night. We had been afraid that he would look down on our little wreck, since his was more than ten times older, but he was quite excited by the samples we showed him—the first genuine treasure he had ever seen.

We left Colombo the next afternoon on what we hoped would be our final attempt to reach the reef. I was getting seriously alarmed about all these delays; if the southwest monsoon was early this year, as was sometimes the case, there would be no hope of doing any diving. The boat might even be trapped on the open, exposed south coast of the island, where good harbors were few and far between.

By the end of the five-hour drive to Tangalle, we had grown to know a lot about Peter and were very happy to have him with us. Apart from being one of the world's very few experts on underwater archaeology (though he would deny this), he was excellent company and possessed an unusual collection of talents. These will emerge later in this book (we were still discovering them when he left), but we were already awed to find that he was either fluent, or could make himself understood, in Japanese, Hawaiian, Tahitian, Turkish, Greek, French, and German. Before he left the island, he was making progress with Sinhalese and had picked up more words than I had in five years.

Ran Muthu and crew were still waiting patiently at Tangalle, but the weather did not look at all promising. It was dull and windy, and the sea was quite choppy; nevertheless, Mike determined to set sail. Even if he could not reach Kirinda, he would put into the next port of call—the small town of Hambantota, roughly at the halfway mark.

As I watched *Ran Muthu* bucking her way out to sea, I was heartily glad that I was not aboard her, and was not at all surprised when she turned back after only fifteen minutes. But the mariners had not been beaten by the weather; one of the engine exhausts had broken, and was belching diesel smoke into the boat. There was nothing to do but to wait at Tangalle, fuming almost as badly as the engine, until we could get a replacement rushed down from Colombo.

The time was not altogether wasted, for Peter set us to work making the tools with which he hoped to map the wreck. Wooden poles were painted in alternating black-and-white one-foot lengths, to act as survey rods, and several dozen large tags were cut out of galvanized zinc and clearly numbered. He proposed to tie these to prominent objects on the seabed, so that he would have some definite reference points when he started making measurements.

By noon the next day, the exhaust had been repaired (so we thought) and *Ran Muthu* got out to sea again, with Mike, Peter, and the two boatmen aboard. We of the shore party waited until they were safely out of sight, in case of any false alarms; then we packed all the rest of the gear, and drove along the coast to Hambantota, where the boat should arrive in the late afternoon. We stopped once at a headland on the way and looked out to sea through the telescope—and there she was, coming along nicely. But when she caught up with us at the harbor, we had bad news. This morning's "repaired" exhaust had broken again.

So we spent the evening at Hambantota, while the "repair" was repaired. This small town, the last place of any size along the south coast of Ceylon, has literary associations of some interest. In the early years of the century, the district was administered by Leonard Woolf, who though not as famous as his wife, Virginia, did publish one novel generally regarded as a classic, *The Village in the Jungle*. The background of this work, which is a most vivid and moving picture of a way of life that has passed only recently, was the jungle around Hambantota.

A local welding shop did such a thorough job on the broken exhaust pipe that we were quite sure it would hold this time. So after a good night's sleep at the fine Hambantota resthouse, Hector and I drove off on the final lap to Kirinda, confident that *Ran Muthu* would catch up with us in a few hours. By then we would have unpacked our equipment and established our shore base, so that everything would be ready when the boat arrived.

At this point, I think it would be a good idea to list the complete cast of our mammoth production, so that you know who was who and what they did. Here it is:

ABOARD THE BOAT

PETER THROCKMORTON	Diver, photographer, archaeologist
MIKE WILSON	Diver, film director
MARTIN	Boatman, general handyman
LAZA	Ditto

WITH THE LAND PARTY

HECTOR EKANAYAKE   Boxer, diver,
photographer, film actor
A. P. PIERIS   Still and movie photographer
MYSELF

Rodney Jonklaas (Diver, marine zoologist) arrived under his own power in his own Volkswagen, and brought with him perhaps the most important man of the expedition—the cook, Anthony.

Our living arrangements were primitive and rugged. We simply moved into the Imperial Lighthouse Service's shed which we shared with the launch *Pharos II* and the staff on shore duty. We had brought some camp beds, but not enough, and the lighthouse staff kindly loaned us spare blankets and cots, and moved into odd corners of the shed to make room for us. When we had unloaded all our aqualung cylinders, cameras, stores, diving gear, personal kit, and so forth, there was very little floor space left.

We were fairly well organized when, in the middle of the morning, *Ran Muthu* came round the rocky headland beneath the shrine, and anchored out in the bay, some two hundred yards from shore. It was not safe to bring her in any closer; if she dragged anchor in the night she could easily go aground on the gently shelving beach, but the invaluable rubber dinghies allowed us to shuttle back and forth without any trouble.

As soon as the crew came ashore, they brought depressing news. Yes—the exhaust had broken yet again. Not in the place mended twice during the last thirty-six hours, but practically everywhere else. The whole system of flexible pipes was coming apart; however, the versatile Peter thought he could fix it, and he worked all afternoon with Martin and Laza in the hot, pitching boat. By nightfall, they had completed the job, as far as it could be done, and came ashore for dinner.

Our patient cook, Anthony, working on the beach with two or three pots and pans and a smoking wood fire that I found it impossible to approach without suffocation, produced a fine meal of fried fish and *iced fruit salad*. For this last miracle, we could again thank Rodney, who has spent so much time in jungles and other god-forsaken places that he has developed a great talent for making himself comfortable. He had brought with him a huge ice box, quite large enough to accommodate unwanted corpses, and we used this to store our perishable food and cold drinks.

I have seldom slept more soundly than on that rough canvas cot, tucked under the side of the lighthouse relief launch, in that shed on Kirinda Beach. Once a passing shower woke me, for I had been unfortunate enough to place my bed immediately under a hole in the roof—but even this seemed only an amusing trifle. Being careful not to disturb the other sleepers, I moved the cot a few inches and, as the rain had stopped almost as soon as it had started, tiptoed out to look at the weather.

It was wonderfully peaceful on the great empty arc of sand, curving away for miles beneath the waning moon. The outrigger fishing boats drawn up on the beach, waiting to depart before dawn, looked strange and mysterious in the pale moonlight. The sea was very calm, and only a few little waves came rippling up to my feet.

Suddenly, far out at sea, a ruby star pulsed once on the horizon. The rotating beams from the Great Basses Lighthouse were sweeping patiently round the sky, as they had done every night for ninety years. I was not the only person awake, here in the small hours before the equatorial dawn; out there one of the lightkeepers was on duty, tending the great lantern in its granite tower a hundred feet above the rocks.

Yes, it was peaceful and lovely now; but what would it be like on this exposed and open bay on a pitch-black, moonless night, when the monsoon gales were howling and the great waves came thundering up the beach? And that time was approaching fast; we would need better luck than we had had so far, if we were to explore that tantalizing wreck. For if we left it too late, the Great Basses would claim one more victim.

Yet I felt content, for we had finally reached Kirinda, with all our equipment, our boat, and our diving team. The treasure, if it existed, was only ten miles away.

15

Through

the Reef

Four hundred miles from the equator, the days and nights are practically the same length the whole year round. The sun always rises at 6 A.M., and sets at 6 P.M., to within a few minutes; there are none of the long summer days or long winter nights that we know in northern latitudes. This gives life a certain monotony; it is completely geared to twelve hours of darkness and twelve hours of light.

We soon adapted ourselves to this routine, and were already moving around in the brief morning twilight before the dawn broke. After a quick breakfast, we checked the gear and loaded it into the rubber boats; before 9 A.M. *Ran Muthu* was on her way to the reef.

Though Mike had pressed me to come, I was not aboard. The boat was already crowded, and on this first day I decided to stay on land. I was still extremely weak, and if anything went wrong I would only be in the way. Moreover, I wanted a full report on conditions at the reef before I would risk going out, even as a sightseer.

There was plenty to do on land. Our activities around the

boathouse had attracted a great deal of local interest; we were probably the most exciting thing that had happened at Kirinda for years. Crowds of curious onlookers watched our every move, and I realized that this might be embarrassing if we did find anything valuable in the wreck. It was hard enough to keep an eye on our equipment, especially as hordes of small children were always hovering around and would not be shooed away. Several items disappeared during our visit—including an aqualung pressure gauge of Rodney's—of no use to anyone else, but invaluable to him. On the whole, however, we did not do badly; if the locals had been so inclined, they could have skinned us clean.

Ceylon is a mixture of many races, the two main groups being the Sinhalese (mostly Buddhist) and the Tamils (mostly Hindu); together, these make up over ninety per cent of the total population. The inhabitants of Kirinda, however, belonged to a small minority group; they were Muslims, and many of them showed clear signs of their Malay origin. During the nineteenth century, a regiment of Malay troops had been disbanded here, and had settled down as farmers and fishermen. Their descendants still spoke Malay, though they all understood Sinhalese and Tamil, and often English as well.

We often wondered what they thought about our activities; though the youngsters were friendly, it was impossible to establish contact with the adults. They stood around watching us, usually without any signs of emotion; but one day a wispy, bleary-eyed elder whom we christened the Mad Mullah stationed himself outside the shed and delivered an impassioned address to anyone who would listen. Whether he was calling upon the Faithful to unite against the infidels who were looting the treasures that rightly belonged to them, we never knew.

On that first morning, I waited until *Ran Muthu* had had time to get out to the reef, and then carried the Questar up to the top of the little hill. There again was the lighthouse gleaming whitely in the sun; there was Shark's Tooth Rock, with the breakers foaming around it. And there, rising and falling above the surf, was *Ran Muthu's* canvas awning.

She was stationed on the landward side of the reef, and through the telescope it was quite hair-raising to see how she appeared to be completely submerged in the boiling surf, every time she sank in the trough of a wave. But I knew that this was an illusion; she was actually several hundred yards from the surf, anchored in relatively smooth water. For the first time I realized the difficulties the divers would be facing; they would have to work right into that line of foam, in the danger area that *Ran Muthu* herself could never approach.

I watched for over an hour from the hilltop, wondering what was happening out there on the horizon. From time to time, far out in the Indian Ocean, an oil tanker or a freighter would go majestically past; this was a very busy spot, and I counted four large ships in half an hour. Usually their hulls were below the horizon, so I had dramatic proof of the fact that the world is round. For I would see only the bridge at the center of a ship, and the superstructure at its stern, moving in splendid isolation along the skyline. At first glance, it would seem as if two separate ships were sailing past—not one, half hidden by the curve of the globe.

At last, late in the afternoon, I saw that *Ran Muthu* was moving away from her anchorage. She made a wide circuit around the boiling water of the reef, then passed in front of the lighthouse as she headed for home.

You can imagine with what eagerness I waited on the shore, when *Ran Muthu* came round the headland and dropped anchor in the bay. I also counted the number of heads on board, and was relieved to find that as many were coming back as had gone out. A few minutes later, the rubber dinghy, chugging along with its little outboard motor, brought the divers back to land.

Peter stepped ashore, staggering under the weight of a

heavy sack, which seemed likely to arouse all sorts of local suspicions. By this time, of course, there was such an enormous crowd that we had to push our way through it to carry the equipment back to the shed—though some of the friendlier young Kirindans helped us with the aqualung cylinders.

We did our best to divert attention from the sack by showing some of the other finds—which were quite surprising. Of all things, Mike and Peter had brought back a large number of empty soda water bottles from the reef.

They weren't like any soda water bottles I'd ever seen before; they had pointed bases, like the ancient amphorae that litter the bottom of the Mediterranean, so they could only lie on their sides. But the biggest surprise, from my point of view, was the raised lettering on the green-tinted glass:

CLARKE-ROMER & CO.

CEYLON

SUPERIOR SODA WATER

It gave me an odd feeling to see my own name emerging from the sea, in this relic of a forgotten marine tragedy. I knew at once, of course, that it had nothing to do with the silver wreck; I felt certain that no one had been bottling soda water around 1702. (Though I was very much surprised to discover that they had started to do so by the end of that same century!) When we had all settled down in the boat shed, Mike and Peter told me what had happened.

Though the sea was very calm when they arrived at the reef, there was a big swell breaking over the exposed rocks. They had anchored *Ran Muthu* in the smoother water on the landward side of the reef; and when the divers had put on their aqualungs and gone down, *there* was a splendid wreck almost immediately beneath them.

It was quite a large ship—about 150 feet long—and had obviously hit the reef from the seaward side and then been carried right over it, to settle down in shallow, fairly sheltered water. It was completely broken up, and seemed to be about a century old—though this could be no more than an educated guess. Besides a mass of ballast stones, the wreck was littered with many badly corroded iron spheres, which looked as if they might be mortar shells. Mike also found some lead plugs, marked with the broad arrow—the official sign of the British government.

But the soda water bottles were the really intriguing items, and we hoped that they would give us a clue to the date of the wreck. Underwater archaeology is like a detective story, and the most trivial items can sometimes lead to important discoveries. Mixed with the soda water bottles there were also many brandy bottles, and Mike and Peter actually retrieved a brandy-and-soda—the two bottles cemented together by coral, unbroken after at least a hundred years on this storm-lashed reef. The brandy bottle still has its cork intact, and contains a dubious amber fluid. We could not help wondering about all this liquor; had it contributed to the wreck?

Interesting though it was, this relatively modern ship was only a diversion from the main objective, and the divers devoted little time to it. Then Mike led them off on the long, hard swim through the reef, to the site that he had last visited with Bobby and Mark two years before.

Mike has an astonishing sense of direction, and he needed it in this complicated and dangerous territory of rocks and gullies, with the surf breaking on all sides. As they got further into the reef, they had to go deep to avoid the foam; there is nothing more terrifying than swimming blind, in seething white water, expecting your face mask to smash against a rock at any moment. At this point there was a convenient cave through the reef which allowed them to take a short cut—and here Rodney's diving career nearly came to an end.

For some time a small amount of water had been coming

through his mouthpiece, but he had ignored it as it did not seem dangerous. However, when he reached the floor of the cave, he found that he was getting no air at all—the mouthpiece was feeding him nothing but seawater. He was barely able to turn back through the cave, swim out under the line of foam, and reach the surface. Rodney himself considers this his narrowest underwater escape; I very much doubt if many other divers would have been able to save themselves.

He swam straight back to the boat, switched to a new regulator, and then went after Mike and Peter again, but was unable to find his way through the gap that only Mike knew. After he had lost his way in a labyrinth of caves, Rodney turned back; so he did not see the wreck that day.

But Mike led Peter straight to the site without a moment's hesitation; here is Peter's description of what they found, as he dictated it that night into my tape recorder down on the deserted beach, with the murmur of the waves providing a soft background noise, and the ruby star of the lighthouse flashing on the horizon every forty-five seconds. Though I have shortened it slightly, I have not attempted to edit or polish the transcript, because I want to preserve the excitement—and the confusion—of the first view of the wreck. Peter's detailed report, written at the end of the expedition in the relative tranquillity of Colombo, will be found in the Appendix.

So over to Peter:

We anchored the boat to the north of the reef, that is, the opposite side from where the swells were breaking, and we swam from the boat to the wreck site, which was probably a mistake because we had to swim through the current, and we used up too much air getting there. Anyway, we got to the site. It was quite surprising for me because there were more fish on that reef than I'd ever seen anywhere in one place, except perhaps in places like Johnson Island and Christmas Island in the

Central Pacific. Anyway, we swam through this—the surf breaking over the ridge of rock—and we swam through cracks, through ways in the rock that Mike knew, into the place where the coin wreck was. It lies between the first ridge of rock, which breaks the south swell, and the main spine of the Great Basses Reef.

It seems very clear what happened to the wreck. The whole site is about sixty feet long. This is just an estimate which could be very wrong. At one end there are two large iron anchors—that is, at the east end. Then, about twenty or thirty feet to the west—this channel between the two ridges in which the wreck lies runs almost due east and west—is a series of cannons. These cannons are jumbled together like matchsticks. I noticed about ten, although I didn't count them, and I noticed very clearly that only one seemed to be a long gun and the others were quite obviously short cannons—cannonades —which is what you would expect in this small ship of war of this period, and, about twenty or thirty feet to the west of the cannons is a smaller brass cannon, about four feet long by a foot in diameter—perhaps smaller. It's bronze or brass and in very good condition, almost completely covered with coral. That brass cannon lies across the channel.

The gully is quite wide. It's about thirty or forty feet wide, or perhaps less, and where the brass cannon lies, the bottom is a mass of concreted corrosion products of iron, bits of silver coins, musket balls and so forth, and lying just above the muzzle of the cannon—which lies in the north and south direction with its muzzle disappearing into the overgrowth of coral—lying above it are two or three pieces of iron, and a mass of generalized corroded mess. I picked out of it the wooden stock of a pistol—still in fairly good condition although just broken off.

I tagged the brass cannon. It's got number 3 on it now.

I tagged a couple of the others also. Well, it seems obvious that the ship sank head down—went over the outer reef, bilged herself hopelessly, and sank right there, and probably went down bow first with her stern up, and hung on the reef, and I should think that the cannons shaking up and down, the whole wreck pounding up and down, and big swells as there must have been when she went on the rocks, the cannons will have shortly jumbled, broken loose from their ring-bolts in the deck, and will have slid down the deck to the position where they now are. The anchors will have fallen off the bows or gone down right with the bows. It's quite apparent that nothing remained of the ship. The whole of the ship was battered, swept off the reef to the north, and the ship ran on the reef, while running before the southwest monsoon. And again, if she'd sunk that way, that explains very easily the small cannon, which must have been gone as it were on the poop, or mounted on the bulwarks, and the brass cannon which might have been aft. I don't know what it was for, but it might have been a signaling gun or something of that sort, kept in the poop, polished up. The heavy brass gun went down and into the gully. The lighter guns were swept off with the shattered bulwarks and poop, as was the cannon which is lying to the north of the wreck, which probably was in the main cabin of the ship. I think ships of that type probably had a chaser gun, a long gun in the cabin, pointing out the stern port. The whole stern window actually could be taken down so they could shoot out of it.

The material around the brass gun in the gully again is the kind of material you'd expect to have come from the lazaret of the ship, which is the obvious place where bullion of any kind would be stored. The pistol handle, the bit of silver bowl, the musket balls and things I forgot to mention—there were cannon balls—must have all come from somewhere in the aft end of the ship, probably underneath the captain's cabin, because under the captain's cabin would probably be the ship's gun room, arms room, where cutlasses, muskets and stuff would be stored and probably near there also in the aft end of the ship, about three-quarters of the way aft in the ship, would have been the powder room with an access into the main hold so that the powder boys could carry the charges to the guns in the waist. I think it's almost certain that the cannon balls were shells. That is why they were hollow spheres of iron with powder inside them. We actually got one out complete and broke another one taking it out, and the wooden plug that was in the iron cannon ball I took out is now sitting in a plastic bag. Again, an analysis of the wood in that plug would give an idea where the ship came from. I got several other wood samples.

So quite obviously when that ship went down she broke up completely; the heavy objects sifted down into the bottom of the gully, and that's where we're finding them now. Everything washed back and forth and stuck in crevices of the rock and jammed there together. Mixed in with this iron material were stones which were like ballast stones. They're of a reddish slatey stone. I suppose some geologist could tell us where a stone of that kind belongs and also tell us where the ship ballasted. We hope that tomorrow when we dive we will find some more definitive material that will help us date the wreck. The bronze cannon is obviously a very good clue to the origin of the wreck. We may be able to dig it out of the coral.

During their first dive, Mike and Peter were chiefly concerned to learn the geography of the wreck, but as Peter described, they managed to chip out an interesting collection of items from the seabed. All this material, mixed up with coral and stones, had been in the sack that Peter had humped ashore; it was not, as I had greedily hoped, a solid mass of silver. But here and there, easy to miss unless you were looking for them, were the little disks of corroded coins. And several were in quite good condition, with their curving Persian script and the familiar date 1113.

It was the right wreck. Despite all that had happened since his last visit, Mike still knew his way through the seething labyrinth of the reef.

16

Valley of

Wrecks

Mike's own account of that first day's diving provides an interesting contrast to Peter's, and fills in some additional details. It also gives a good foretaste of the dangers which we were to meet in working on this site, and some of the steps that had to be taken to overcome them. Mike speaking:

We were always debating exactly where we were going to anchor on the reef; because of the big surge and the currents, we weren't very sure how safe it was going to be. But I'd always had in mind to use the anchor from what I'd thought to be a 1765 Dutch wreck that Major Raven-Hart told us about;[1] I figured we could take a chain from that to a buoy on the surface and then just

---

[1] This refers to the sloop *Aletta Adriana,* carrying Lt. Groose, lost in late 1765 or early 1766 on her way from Trincomalee to Colombo. It is one of the few specific references to wrecks on the Great Basses that Major Raven-Hart was able to locate for us in a search he made at the Ceylon Archives, Nuwara Eliya. An apparently much more promising reference dated 1704 (cf. the 1702 of our coins) to the loss of the "Flute *Overness*" on the Great Basses, has so far led nowhere. We have located no fewer than three *Overnesses,* but they were laid up in 1717, 1770 and 1772!

tie up there whenever we wanted to come to the reef.

The day we got out there, it was very calm; a little bit of a chop, but quite calm by Basses standards, and we anchored over the top of the wreck. Rodney found the wreck, and went into the water. The wreck was much closer to the reef than I'd imagined before, and we anchored right over it and *Ran Muthu* held fast. And then due to a weird tidal or current movement, she lay back towards the reef. I was rather nervous about leaving the boat, but we lay there for a while, about half an hour, before we got into the water; she bounced around a bit, but she held solidly, and it was obvious that she was not going to move unless very bad weather came up. So we all harnessed up, went down, and pottered about this wreck underneath us, using it as an assembly point. As soon as we'd assembled there, we started to swim for the reef underwater.

Well, this in itself was a mistake, and yet it wasn't a mistake. We could have gone on snorkel, but I think we'd have been much tireder. Since we swam the distance, we used up quite a lot of air. We came up close under the reef, because I wanted to get Peter acquainted with conditions as soon as possible—and they were pretty hairy because the break was coming over and obscuring everything with white water.

We got down on the bottom, hanging on, pulling ourselves forward. The water was very, very clear and I could see Peter. I stayed a little ahead of him, leading the way. Rodney didn't come and we learned later that he'd turned back because of a defective regulator. We hung on there for about two or three minutes, waiting for Rodney, but we were getting thrown around by the surge, I mean *really* thrown around, up in the air and all over the show. So I decided to go through the reef.

Now at this point, the reef sides are sheer, going to a

scooped depression about thirty-five feet deep. As you go up the reef wall, about six feet below the surface, you come to a narrow gap which runs almost directly through the reef, and there are barnacle-encrusted rocks to which you can hang on to. The surf was moderate at this point, and so I waited for the right moment, and went through the gap, expecting Peter to follow me. He tried several times, but got thrown down. So I came back over the reef again and then demonstrated the method of getting through the reef to him. And the second time he came through, I managed to get a grip on the rock, and together we got through to the deeper water.

I very quickly recognized the plateau where we found the second bronze cannon two years previously, and led Peter right to the spot. It hadn't changed much. I swam the whole length of the wreck with Peter, showing him the cannon, the anchors, and finally, the place where we'd found the silver. We poked around there a bit, and then Peter gave me an indication that his air was off. So I went back with him to the surface, by that time Laza had rowed the dinghy around the reef, and was holding station.

Now I should mention that previously as soon as Laza came around, I sent him right back again to get some more air; so that by the time we came back to the spot with our air exhausted, Laza was waiting with some more compressed air. We went aboard the dinghy and tanked up and went down, still asking where Rodney was. Rodney apparently had got discouraged and was not sure where we were, so he was staying close to *Ran Muthu*. We dived around a bit and since we had such a long swim, about two hundred yards, through very hard conditions, we didn't feel much like carrying anything back with us. We had a very good look at the site, made some measurements, drove some pitons in, left some equipment on the spot, and we came back with Laza in the dinghy around the reef to the *Ran Muthu*, still anchored over the other wreck.

Up until now, this wreck had been very interesting to us because we thought it might have been the 1765 one that Major Raven-Hart had told us about. We went down and very soon the modern anchor design told us that this wasn't the case at all. Then I found cases of bottles which I opened up; I looked at the name engraved on the bottles and took one over and pointed it out to Peter. He gave a nod, and we knew then that the Clarke-Romer, Ceylon, Soda Water wreck, or the brandy-and-soda wreck as we came to call it, would date from about 1850 or 1860.

It was a very interesting little wreck, and we stayed over it for the rest of the day, giving it a good picking over. There was a tremendous amount of material in the wreck—mortar shells, for instance—and we found some caps for the mortar shells, lead caps with the broad arrow of the War Department on them. We found the base of a silver candlestick and lots of other things. It does bear a lot of future diving—that particular wreck.

So we came back to the land, fairly happy with the day's diving.

That first evening back from the reef set the pattern of all those to follow. We would unload and check the cameras, start pumping up the empty aqualung cylinders, see that *Ran Muthu* was securely anchored, and do all the dozens of other odd jobs which are necessary to keep an underwater expedition functioning. The center of interest, however, was Peter.

He would sit at a bench, covered with the dirty, smelly

masses of rock that he and Mike had salvaged from the bottom of the sea, and chip patiently away at them for hour
after hour. From time to time something of interest would
emerge from the coral, and he would drop it into one of the
many little tins and boxes he had set up.

To most people, the objects he was collecting would
hardly have seemed of much value or importance; to the
archaeologist, they were vital, for any one of them might
provide the essential clue which would allow us to identify
the wreck. Perhaps the most interesting and romantic item
was a complete pistol stock, the wood quite sound, but the
metal of the barrel almost entirely rusted away. It was one
of a pair (the second was badly broken up) and the brass
plates covering the butts were in perfect condition, inscribed
with handsome floral designs.

Peter also collected small fragments of wood from the site
of the wreck, and sealed them in plastic bags to prevent them
from disintegrating when they dried out. He hoped that
experts might be able to identify, not only the type of wood,
but even the part of the world where it had grown. In this
way, we might be able to discover where the ship was built.

From time to time, as Peter chipped his patient way
through the lumps of coral, one of the Mogul rupees would
come to light. Since all Peter's operations were watched by
a large crowd of spectators, we thought that the best thing
to do was to show these frankly, and to explain what they
were, but to make no particular fuss about them. If we tried
to hide them, that in itself would look suspicious. For, after
all, one would expect to find *some* coins in an old wreck. We
hoped that it would be obvious to our audience that we
weren't going to make any fortunes this way, chipping out
one or two rupees an hour.

It was while we were doing this that, strangely enough,
the shadow of the most famous treasure hunt of modern
times fell across our little group. The lighthouse superin-

tendent, Frank Rees, came to see how we were getting on; and he told us of his adventures on the evening of May 20, 1922.

He had been aboard the 8,000–ton P. & O. liner *Egypt*, steaming through thick fog off the French coast on her way from London to Bombay. Suddenly, out of the mist, came the bows of a cargo steamer; the *Egypt* was struck amidships and sank in twenty minutes. Ninety-six people went down with her—plus seven tons of gold and silver.

Frank Rees was lucky; he walked off the deck straight into the water as the ship sank, and was picked up two hours later, covered with oil and black with soot. When he arrived at Brest, it took him some time to convince the French that he was not one of the *Egypt's* native crew. All this happened to him on his twenty-first birthday; few youngsters can have had so memorable a coming-of-age.

The *Egypt* and her gold lay in four hundred feet of water —beyond the practical working depth of conventional diving gear even today. However, an Italian team with the salvage vessel *Artiglio* developed observation chambers and grabs, and set out to recover the £1,045,000 lying at the bottom of the Bay of Biscay.

It took years of searching even to locate the wreck, and then it was necessary to blast a way into her interior, using explosives to cut a way through, deck after deck, until the strong room was reached. Weather conditions were so bad that work was possible only for a few weeks in every year, and while they were engaged upon another salvage job, the divers accidentally touched off thousands of tons of explosives in a sunken munitions ship. *Artiglio* and her crew went down in a man-made tidal wave.

But the work continued next year (1931) with *Artiglio II*, and soon the grabs started bringing up gold bars and sovereigns. When operations ended in 1935, more than 95 per cent of the *Egypt's* bullion had been recovered, from the greatest depth at which salvage had ever been attempted. The price had been almost ten years of work and a dozen lives—a good reminder of the tenacity with which the sea holds its treasures.

It had been through Frank Rees's cooperation that Mike had discovered our wreck, for Frank had given us permission to use the lighthouse as a base on our earlier expeditions. This was his last visit to Kirinda, as he was about to retire; we were very happy to be able to give him some of our finds to take back to England as souvenirs of the Great Basses. When we sat on the beach that evening, listening to his tales (the *Egypt* had not been his only shipwreck), I was irresistibly reminded of Millais' *The Boyhood of Rayleigh*. As in that famous painting, Mike, Peter and I were all gathered around Frank's feet like eager schoolboys, while he sat on an overturned boat and told us of his forty years at sea. We wish him well in the quiet of England, far from the realm of the monsoon.

17

View from

the Dinghy

The next morning, the sea was very calm and the sun was shining brilliantly in a clear sky. I would never have a better opportunity of watching the divers at work; so this time, I was aboard *Ran Muthu* when she sailed.

The outrigger fishing boats, the cluttered shed that we had made our temporary home, the whitely gleaming shrine on its hilltop overlooking Kirinda, all fell slowly astern as we chugged out to sea. After an hour's run, the coast of Ceylon seemed very far away, and the tower of the lighthouse was looming up ahead, dominating the horizon.

It was about here that I lost my breakfast; I am normally quite a good sailor, but I had found a sure-fire recipe for seasickness. It is to concentrate on taking photographs through the finder of a Leica, aboard a slowly pitching boat. Waiting for that horizon to come horizontal is a good test for any stomach.

When we got to the reef, Mike took the boat carefully and cautiously round it and anchored this time on the seaward side, about a hundred yards from the breakers. He did not propose to swim through those coral caves again.

Rodney, Mike, and Peter put on their aqualungs, and dropped overboard. I remember my gasp of astonishment when they submerged, and I saw how startingly brilliant the colors on their clothes and equipment remained as they sank down into the water. I had quite forgotten how pure and transparent this ocean water could be, and its crystal depths looked very attractive. I no longer had any hesitation about going in, though I did not feel strong enough to handle an aqualung; I much preferred to make my first dive unencumbered.

Putting on flippers, face mask, gloves, and weight belt, I gripped the snorkel tube between my teeth, and lowered myself into the water. I was taking no chances at all, but hung on to the side of the rubber dinghy while Laza rowed it over to the reef, to join the other divers.

The view beneath me, though wonderfully clear, was not very impressive. I was snorkeling across a rocky seabed with no coral and little marine growth, and very few fish. But as I approached the reef, the underwater terrain became much more rugged, dropping away into numerous pits and gullies.

I also began to feel the first ominous tug of the swell that was surging over the reef, even on this calm day. Laza brought the rubber dinghy to rest about fifty feet away from the line of foam, and some two hundred feet from *Ran Muthu*. He would keep station here, so that if the divers got into trouble, they would find help at once as soon as they surfaced. However, it was not safe even for the dinghy to remain too near the wreck site; Laza had to keep his distance, and watch out for any sudden waves that might surge up and sweep him on to the reef.

As soon as the dinghy came to a halt, I could see the divers at work, though they were still fifty feet away and thirty feet down. Hanging on to a rope from the dinghy—I was being ultra cautious, and with good reason—I swam over to them and had a perfect bird's eye view of operations.

The first thing I noticed was the small cannon, half buried in the coral that had grown around it during two and a half centuries. (Coral can do far better than that, but on this exposed and wave-swept site it had made very slow progress—luckily for us.) There was nothing else that would have caught my eye, had I been swimming casually across this section of the reef.

Rodney's fine "aerial" photograph (Fig. 40) gives an excellent idea of the seabed around the cannon, but this depicts only part of one small valley in the reef. Other valleys, deeper and more mysterious, led away in all directions, their details becoming lost in the blue haze a hundred feet away. Toward the reef itself, the foaming water created a white, sparkling fog—a deadly mist that surged up and down with every passing swell.

There was a lot of activity down there on the seabed. Mike was chipping away, with hammer and chisel, at the half-exposed cannon, while Peter was swimming along the wreck unrolling a tape measure. He was engaged in the very difficult but important operation of mapping the site, by measuring the distance between the numbered metal tags he had wired to prominent objects such as anchors and cannon.

Nothing could sound easier; but listen to Peter's account of the operation:

I was continually getting tangled up with the tape. We built a kind of anchor at one end of it while I hung on the other end, and I found that all the cannons seemed to be the same length. The measured length, including the sea growth, is eight to eight and a half feet. The variation is because I was getting washed around when I was making the measurements. Where I was measuring, you can't even swim from one end of the site to the other. You have to hold on tight to the bottom while the opposing current runs by you, and then, when the current is running your way, let go and be swept by the current to where you want to go and hold on when it stops. You have half a minute of lull, and then it sweeps the other way. I was banged all over. Once I caught my swim-fin in a crack in the rock, while I was being dragged in the opposite direction by the current, and thought my leg was being broken. I lost my grip half a dozen times and once was swept twenty or thirty feet completely out of control, but I discovered that, like everything else, this is something that you can get used to. Though it's very unpleasant and difficult, it is possible to work in that place. For instance, when I was swept, I just hunched over and made sure that my air bottle hit the coral cliff behind me. Mike said that he heard me going "clang, clang" periodically as the seas crashed over the reef.

Because I was careful not to get too far from the dinghy, I kept clear of this disturbed water, and was able to study the situation at leisure. As I gazed around, my eyes learned to see more and more details in the confused jumble beneath me. What at first appeared to be random piles of stone or coral, the products of purely natural causes, slowly shaped themselves into meaningful patterns.

If you study Fig. 40, you can go through the same process —in considerably more comfort that I did. Here Peter is hovering over the bronze cannon, which he has tagged with the metal label painted "1." Some of his equipment is lying around him: crowbars, pitons, deflated *Port-A-Lift* balloon (see next chapter), snorkel, and Calypso camera (face down by the breech of the cannon).

At first sight, the seabed around the cannon looks perfectly natural; but it is not. There are lines, circles, and lumps in its mottled patterns which are not entirely the work of coral and monsoon. At the center of the photograph, almost touching the snorkel, is one of the most interesting of these artifacts— a light circle with a concentric dark circle inside.

Mark Smith and Bobby Kriegel had observed this on their

first dive, two years before. It is a large glass object, almost completely buried in the seabed. I had questioned Mark about it immediately after his return from the reef, with these results:

CLARKE   Bobby mentioned that he saw a peculiar glass object, half buried in the sand. Have you any idea what it was?

MARK   I don't have any idea, no. But it was pretty well buried.

CLARKE   How big was it?

MARK   It was about the size of—so big around. (*Gestures.*)

CLARKE   (*Trying to remind Mark that this is a sound, not vision, recording.*) That's about four inches across?

MARK   Yes, and then the outside walls are about *that* big. (*Gestures again.*)

CLARKE   (*Still trying.*) That would be about the size of a football or even a bit bigger than that?

MARK   Yes. It was perfectly round.

CLARKE   Was it hollow? Did you see the inside of it?

MARK   No. I didn't see inside it. I examined it and it was definitely made out of glass.

CLARKE   What color glass?

MARK   It was a sort of brownish glass.

So once again, as in the case of the brandy and soda from the wreck on the other side of the reef, we have an example of the vagaries of the sea. Here was a large glass object, perhaps a bottle of some kind, still apparently intact after two and a half centuries on an exposed and storm-swept ridge of rock. Now that the coral has grown around it, it is probably safe indefinitely. Mike and Peter, in the limited time they had, could not have removed it without damage. So it is still there, awaiting the next expedition.

Although I was fifty feet from the edge of the reef, at the

outer edge of the disturbed water, the continual rise and fall of the swell presently brought on another mild attack of sea-sickness. So I got Laza to row me over to *Ran Muthu* while I flippered behind him, holding on with one hand. Then he hurried back to the divers while I relaxed, weak but very happy, on the deck of the boat. At least I had *seen* the site, and that made all the difference. The descriptions I had heard now began to make sense, and I could understand the problems that the divers were facing. It now seemed even more incredible to me that, two years ago, Mike and the two boys had been able to work here, at such a distance from their base on the lighthouse—*and* without a boat. They had been lucky enough to catch a brief spell of abnormally calm weather; otherwise their feat would have been quite im-possible.

An hour later, Peter and Mike rejoined me on the boat; Rodney, having taken a series of photographs with his Rolleimarine still camera, was paying a call on the lighthouse keepers, who seldom had visitors and were glad of the un-expected company.

"Well," I asked eagerly, "what about the treasure?"

The answer was disappointing.

"I think we got most of it last time," said Mike. "There doesn't seem to be much more."

Curiously enough, in a way I felt a certain relief. This meant the end of our main worries, as well as of hopes that we had never let ourselves take too seriously. Now at least we could turn our attention to some other project, and leave this dangerous and exhausting work to the professional archaeologists like Peter, who seemed to thrive on it.

After hot cocoa and a few biscuits (in that blazing heat no one felt hungry, and it is unwise to eat much in the mid-dle of a day's diving), Mike and Peter went back to the wreck. I decided not to run any more risks but to stay qui-etly on deck for the rest of the afternoon. My only regret was that, though I had seen the wreck, I had not actually reached it. Perhaps I should have put on an aqualung—but it was too late now. I had no intention of ever going back.

Then, in the middle of the afternoon, the whole situation altered. We had now arranged a shuttle service with the two dinghies, one remaining always near the divers while the other ferried spare tanks and equipment between *Ran Muthu* and the site. Around 2 P.M. Peter came rowing back, and I am never likely to forget his first words to me: "I've found the mother lode. There's at least a ton there."

There was no need for explanations; I knew exactly what he meant.

18

The Mother Lode

Peter hurried back to the site with a new aqua-lung cylinder, and I waited on *Ran Muthu* with what patience I could. Presently Mike arrived in the rubber dinghy; he had been at the lighthouse with Rodney, so knew nothing of Peter's discovery.

When he heard my news, he grabbed a new lung and hurried over to the reef. A good hour passed, while the only sign of activity at the wreck site was Laza paddling back and forth, keeping an eye open for menacing swells. Then, at long last, I saw the two divers surface beside the dinghy, and it started to head back toward *Ran Muthu*.

As it approached, I saw that it was towing an extremely heavy load, partly supported in the water by an ingenious device that Peter had brought with him. This was the Port-A-Lift—a kind of underwater balloon, which a diver can carry down in his pocket, and inflate with air from his regulator. (See Fig. 43.)

The Port-A-Lift was sinking under the weight of a canvas sack, and it took the combined efforts of everyone on the boat to haul it over the side. I remember thinking, as I photographed the scene furiously, "I hope to God the sack doesn't tear open!" Then it "thunked" on to the deck, and Peter carefully lifted out the contents.

139

One by one, massive cylinders of lime-encrusted silver coins emerged from the sack. Each was about the same weight—roughly thirty pounds. Though they were so gray and corroded that no one would have noticed them if they had been lying in a rubbish heap, to us they looked beautiful. For we knew that, beneath the protective outer layer of metal and coral, the silver was still as clean and bright as when it had left the mint of Surat, when Emperor Aurangzeb ruled two and a half centuries ago. Not that anyone would ever see it again, for these perfect 1,000-coin masses were such novelties that it would be an archaeological crime to break them up. Probably nowhere else in the world—except for that one specimen we had donated to the Smithsonian, and those still in the chest back in Colombo—did complete sacks of Mogul rupees exist, just as they had been sealed up in the counting house thirty years before George Washington was born.

Mike, I suspect, was a little upset because Peter had made the first big discovery of the expedition; at least, his account lacks the enthusiasm that a hundredweight of silver would seem to justify. But, as you will see, he was after even bigger game: here is his version of that eventful April 14, 1963, which I got him to record, several months later, in a spare moment snatched from the production of his latest movie. (For *Ranmuthu Duwa* has turned out to be only the first of a series of Sinhalese epics.)

Mike:

We got on the site fairly early this day, around about 9:30, and we worked consistently throughout the day examining the area. This time, though, we started to dig. It's very hard to resist digging, even when you know it should be done fairly scientifically. But the wind was coming up and there was still some swell, so we thought we might not have much more time. So we dug and dug

and dug, and we got a lot of loose coins. Peter used to
pick up the most remarkable lumps of stone, ballast—
stuff which I would just never have bothered with. I was
rather annoyed at this because I felt we could be actually
chipping out silver.

Of course, when we got back to the land, and he
started breaking them open and we found lots of little
things which we might have missed just scratching for
silver, the whole wreck began to take on a different com-
plection. We began to see that if we could find more than
silver, we could find perhaps cutlery, maybe even a
watch, navigating instruments, table ware, any number
of things which would provide a kind of break in the
routine from just collecting money, and give us a better
insight into the wreck itself.

I searched hard for the wall of silver; this was an impression that Bobby Kriegel, Mark Smith and I had got
on our first trip there—that a whole side of the reef wall
was silver. And even today I'm not convinced that this is
not the case, because subsequently I began to search
way, way out from the main site, and I found scattered
coins, as far away to the northeast as a hundred feet, and
still parts of the gunroom equipment. Up on the side of
the wall where we thought we'd seen the silver, I came
across a big plate, piles of cannon balls, and scattered
silver coins once more. I went right over the reef, down
the other side into a small pothole, looking for silver,
though I didn't find any on that side. I thought we'd
pretty much cleared the place out and I was not too
happy with the way the boat was going, so my morale
was at a fairly low ebb.

Presently I came up as I'd run out of air; Rodney had
also run out of air—Peter was still down with the twin-
set aqualung. I took Rodney in the rubber dinghy, with
the outboard motor, and dropped him off near the light-

house to do some spearfishing. By the time I got back to the boat, Peter had been aboard and I was greeted with that grin that Arthur has when he's happy about something. Peter, apparently, had just come up, out of air, having found what we called the mother-lode.

When I joined him, he said, "Well, I've found it. There's more there." I said, "What, the mother-lode?" He said, "That's it." I said, "How much is there?" He said, "A ton at least." Well, I couldn't believe this. Well I believed it, but it was still unbelievable! I didn't see how we could have missed it. But Peter gave me very accurate descriptions of where he'd found the stuff. He said, "Look, I'm tired. You go down and get up what you can." So I went down and brought up four big bags of a different shape than the type we'd found up to now, like large sausages, elongated instead of squat.

This was fairly exciting; it brought our take up to a substantial amount. The question that remained with me all the time was: How far spread out is the wreck? I'm inclined to believe that most of the sand in that area covers silver, either spread out very thinly, or compacted in lumps.

That day's diving would have been enough to satisfy most people; but as long as there was any air left in the tanks, Mike and Peter weren't going home. So they returned to the site, to continue digging away, while I brooded thoughtfully over those sausage-shaped lumps drying out in the sun.

Meanwhile, Rodney had also had a successful afternoon, bringing back a splendid thirty-five pound red snapper which would solve our food problems for the next couple of days. Treasure was all very well, but we could not eat it.

When we hauled up the anchor at 4 P.M. and started back for the mainland, we were all very happy. But now at last we were faced with the problem which, so far, had been only

Fig. 32. Rodney and author on the Great Basses Reef, preparing to dive off the edge.

Mike Wilson

Fig. 33. A new crew for the lighthouse.

Fig. 34. Through the reef.

Mike Wilson

Fig. 35. A perfect day for tunafish sandwich.

Rodney Jonklaas, B. Sc.

Mike Wilson

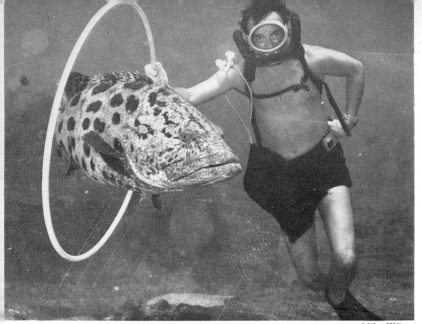

Fig. 36. Rodney puts Ali Baba through his paces.

Fig. 37. An inquisitive shark comes to look at the cameraman.

Mike Wilson

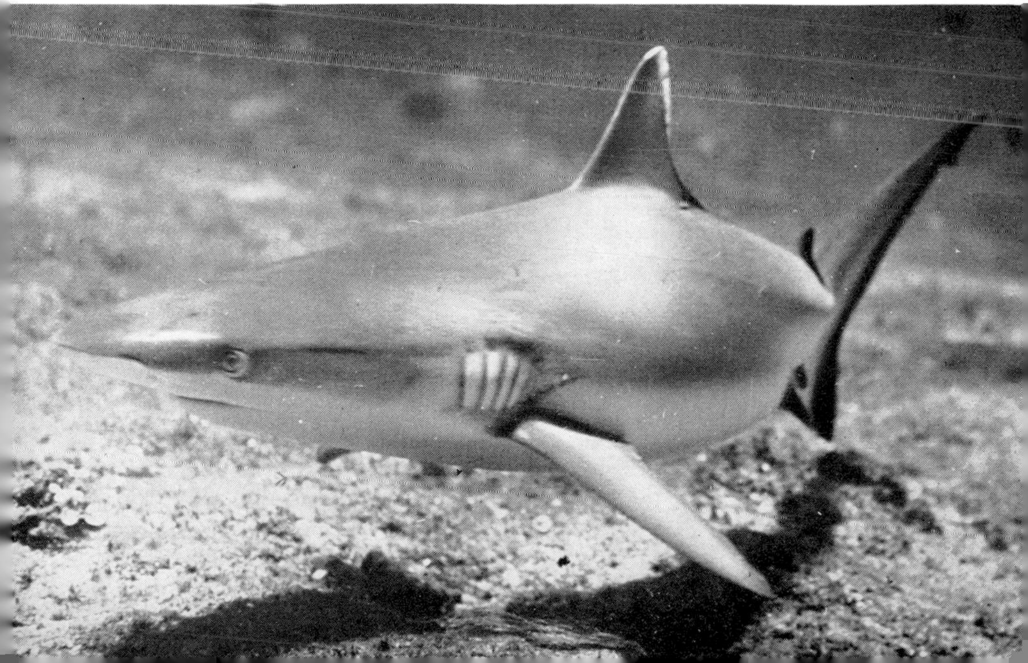

Mike Wilson

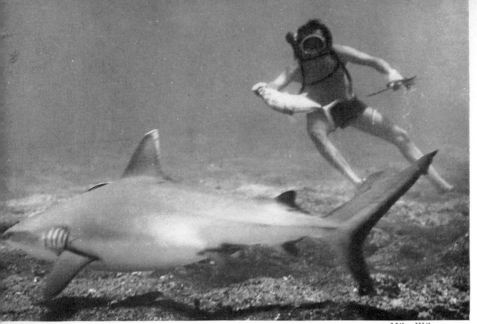

Fig. 38. A hungry shark tries to get at Rodney's fish.

Fig. 39. Mark Smith and Ali Baba.

Mike Wilson

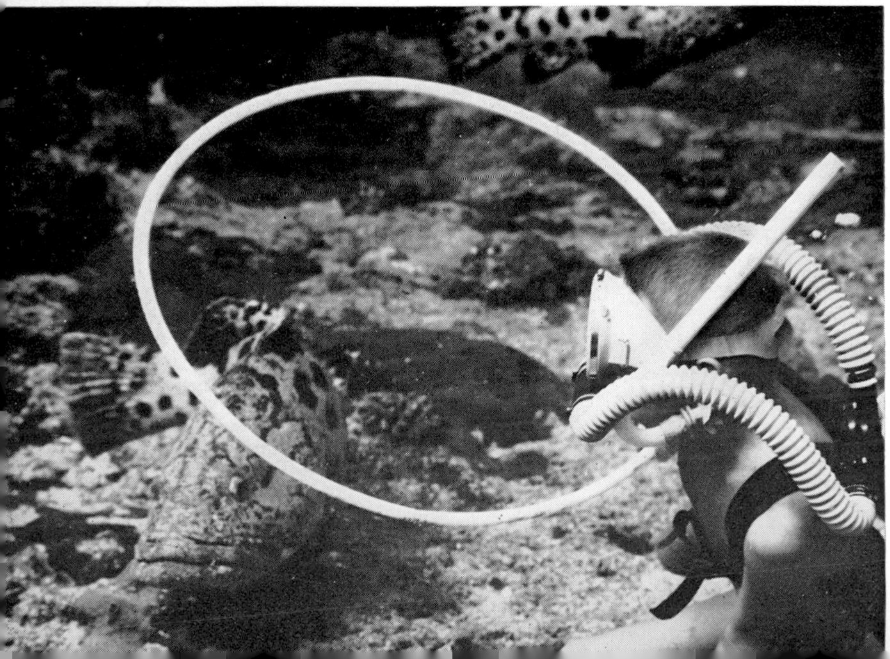

Fig. 40. General view of wreck site, Peter working over bronze cannon.

Fig. 41. Mike films Peter, examining the pile of cannon at the center of the wreck.

Rodney Jonklaas, B. Sc.

Fig. 42. Bobby Kriegel lifts one of the coin masses; even under water, the thirty-pound lump is hard to handle. This may be the first photo ever taken showing sunken treasure at the moment of recovery.

Mike Wilson

Fig. 43. The bronze cannon, freed from the coral, with Port-A-Lift balloon.

Rodney Jonklaas, B. Sc.

Fig. 44. The bronze cannon goes up, guided by Mike.

Rodney Jonklaas, B. Sc.

Rodney Jonklaas, B. Sc.

Fig. 45. Two fish wait hopefully for tidbits while Peter digs into the coral.

Fig. 46. Anchor from mid-nineteenth century wreck.

Rodney Jonklaas, B. Sc.

Fig. 47. Bobby Kriegel (left) and Mark Smith with their finds on the Great Basses lighthouse, photographed on the day of the discovery of the wreck (March 23, 1961).

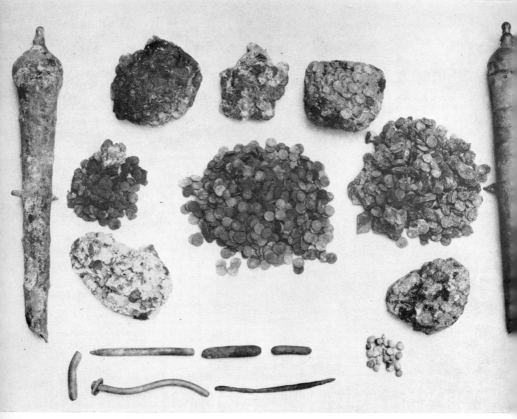

Fig. 48. All the 1961 finds. The coin mass at upper right is now in the Smithsonian Institution, Washington.

Fig. 49. Mike examines the treasure; lighthouse crane in background.

Bobby Kriegel

Fig. 50. Another underwater mystery. Mike and Gamini Fonseka, star of his movie *Ranmuthu Duwa,* haul ashore stone column found off Swami Rock, Trincomalee.

Fig. 51. Coins after cleaning; note (right) Muslim date, 1113 (= 1702 A.D.).

Fig. 52 The bronze cannon after rough cleaning. Scale in inches.

Fig. 53. Copper serving plate from wreck; scale in centimeters.

Fig. 54. Wooden pistol stock; almost all the iron has disappeared, but the wood is still sound. The thimble has been removed from the butt. (See Fig. 56.)

Fig. 55. Close-up of swivel-gun breech, showing ornamentation.

Fig. 56. Bronze thimbles from butts of paired pistols. (Note floral designs.) Fragment of money chest, showing coin and piece of bag. Bronze pestle.

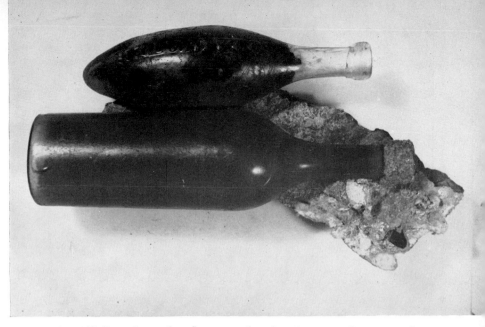

Fig. 57. Brandy and soda water bottles, intact and cemented together by coral, from mid-nineteenth century wreck.

Fig. 58. The first four coin masses aboard *Ran Muthu*.

Fig. 59. Elizabeth shows Tony Wilson ten times his own weight of silver. This photograph shows all the specie recovered by the 1961 and 1963 expeditions, except for mass donated to the Smithsonian.

Fig. 60. Rodney and Peter examine the finds in the Kirinda boat shed.

theoretical. Just what should we do with the treasure we had salvaged?

If we brought it ashore, under all those inquisitive eyes, there might be trouble. In any case, there was nowhere in the lighthouse shed that we could safely leave it. We decided—though this too involved some risks—that the best move would be to hide it under the tools and general junk in one of the obscurest of *Ran Muthu's* many lockers.

So that is what we did. We brought all the other finds ashore, and made a great display of them to the usual evening audience. As Peter dug and tapped his way through the lumps of coral, he found one poignant relic—part of a lady's earring, of a kind still seen in northern India to this day. It made the wreck come suddenly to life across the centuries, linking us to the unknown crew whose hopes and dreams had foundered with her.

Late that night, before settling down to a long and undisturbed sleep beside the hull of the *Pharos II*, I went down to the beach to check that *Ran Muthu* was riding safely at anchor. The storm lantern lashed to her superstructure looked a very faint and distant star out there in the darkness, and it seemed most unlikely that anyone would row out, board her, force the padlock, and find the treasure hidden inside. The silver was safer there than on land—unless, by some irony of fate, *Ran Muthu* sank in the night and restored it once more to the bed of the Indian Ocean.

19

The Bronze Cannon

I was up before sunrise and went down to the beach, to reassure myself that *Ran Muthu* was still riding safely at anchor. There she was, bobbing around out in the bay in the pale pre-dawn light—the only ship in all the world carrying sunken treasure in her lockers. I hoped that she could keep her secret until the expedition was over.

Although Mike wanted me to come out again, I decided that this would be tempting Providence. Not only was I tired and sunburnt after yesterday's exertions, but I had been suffering from agonizing, and rather frightening, cramps in my arms, hands, and neck. These were certainly due to the efforts that my still partly paralyzed muscles had made when I was diving, clinging to the boat as she swayed in the water, and so on. They were probably a very good sign (if a muscle could hurt, I argued, it was trying to work again), but prudence demanded that I take a day's rest. Besides, there was shopping to do; Rodney's magnificent icebox was running out of ice.

So when *Ran Muthu* had set sail to the reef, Hector drove me the thirty miles to Hambantota where we purchased the necessary provisions. Halfway back, in the late afternoon, we were driving along a luckily empty road when there was a grinding crash, the Oxford van "juddered" back and forth across the road surface, and lurched to a halt in the ditch. The front suspension had broken.

We sat and cursed for a few minutes, then climbed out and waited for some Good Samaritan to come to our aid. As we were only five miles from the small but important town of Tissamaharama where there were several well-equipped garages, we were more annoyed than worried by the disaster.

Of course, for the first fifteen minutes all the cars were going in the wrong direction, but then a bus trundled by and we flagged it to a stop. Some years ago, the island's privately owned bus companies were nationalized, and a Ceylon Transport Board was set up with a flourish of trumpets. Unfortunately, the board lacked sufficient vehicles and drivers, and before long private enterprise was back in the field. So now the island has two road transport systems—the CTB, and a whole network of "pirate" buses operating in the shadow of the law, but tolerated because they fill a vital need.

It was one of these pirates that took me to Tissamaharama, while Hector stood guard over the collapsed Oxford. But when I arrived at Tissa, I was shattered to discover that everything was closed. It was the Sinhalese New Year; we could not possibly have chosen a worse day to have a breakdown.

I was wondering what to do next when a very efficient Muslim gentleman took charge of me and started making phone calls in all directions. Despite the holiday, in next to no time he had contacted a mechanic, and rounded up emergency transport. Mr. Mohammed was apologetic about the incredibly ancient Plymouth that rattled into life at our approach, but I was happy to have anything on wheels.

We crept out of Tissa with a sound as of a hundred coffee grinders, and I was acutely conscious of the fact that the bare metal under my feet was slowly becoming red hot. So I kept my fingers crossed, and tried to enjoy the free vibromassage I was getting.

When we reached the Oxford, I was astonished to find that the mechanic had already arrived with his breakdown truck. When Hector started to load our stores into the Plymouth, we found that Rodney's coffin-sized icebox wouldn't go through the side door. So we simply prized off the back of the van (it was only held on by a few nails, and could be as easily replaced), and then rattled off to Kirinda, wondering if we would make it this time. This little episode had practically exhausted my dwindling supply of twentieth century rupees, and I was beginning to wonder if Mogul currency would be accepted by the local tradesmen.

It was dusk when we got back to Kirinda, and *Ran Muthu* had already anchored. She at least had had a successful day; for there on the floor of the shed was the beautiful bronze cannon I had seen the day before, buried in the coral of the reef. It had taken two days' hard work to get it up with the help of an unusual underwater tool—an auto jack. Here is Peter's account of the operation, dictated into the tape recorder that same night:

> The stern of the ship apparently went down where we've been working, and the central point of that area is the brass cannon that we managed to remove today. This area is quite obviously the lazaret of the ship, the stern part of the ship, which contains the powder room, the gun room, and the lazaret underneath the captain's cabin, where the money was usually stored in ships of this period. . . . Yesterday, I began chipping through a concreted mass of hardened tar, gunpowder, the corrosion products of iron, all packed into a kind of stonelike material. . . . Nothing was lying in any special order, though included in the mess were musket barrels, the stock of a pistol, bits of iron and hand grenades—hollow spheres of iron with the wooden plugs still in them. Going through this at the end of my dive, I noticed two sacks of silver concreted together.
>
> We decided that the brass cannon was lying right in the middle of all this gun room material, and it was es-

sential to raise the cannon for two reasons. One, that raising it would loosen up all that material so that we could get under it and see if there were any more sacks of silver coins. And the second reason was that it was a conspicuous thing and marked the wreck. Obviously, it was not advisable to leave a signpost there for somebody to see.

So we worked on our own, after Mike raised the silver yesterday, in chipping loose the concreted mass of stuff around this cannon. It was again tar, corrosion products of iron, bits of ballast stones, bits of splintered wood, the whole thing washed, smashed into a mass, packed into that crevice in the rock by the action of the waves which, when the wave breaks overhead from the south swell, run very strongly east and west in the crevice. So we worked yesterday—the last dive yesterday—on breaking loose the coral rock from around the cannon—tried to raise it without much luck.

I worked getting scattered silver bits chipped off, chipping in the places where there seemed to be three or four rupees cemented together, and all the time working down under the cannon. Finally, we had a place big enough so we could put in the jack; then I placed a heavy sledge hammer on a solid piece of rock under the breech of the cannon, and using a chisel as a wedge, began pounding it between the rock and the sledge, while Mike levered with the auto jack. With those tons of pressure, the cannon broke loose, and we were very happy.

But chipping the cannon out of its coral tomb was only half the problem, even though it had taken the best part of two days. It had to be lifted onto *Ran Muthu,* which was several hundred feet away on the other side of a ridge of underwater hills.

This was where the Port-A-Lift came in handy, but it could support only about a hundred pounds, and the cannon weighed at least three times as much. Here is Rodney's account of the operation, which he photographed from all angles:

We had rather a hectic time getting the cannon off the bottom. Mike was doing this with the aid of the Port-A-Lift and we hitched both dinghies over the spot and tied three main ropes on the cannon. Peter very ably directed operations which enabled us to take the cannon a few feet off the bottom, where Mike could help us by pushing it over the rocks and reefs towards the sea. Once the ropes were shortened considerably, we got the little outboard motor started on one of the dinghies and chugged our way, the cannon bumping along the bottom, but with great luck we managed to get it over the various jagged boulders and reefs and out into deeper water, where of course the dinghy motor flatly refused to work from lack of fuel.

We then lowered the cannon to the bottom of the sea, and left one dinghy on the spot. Then we went back to the boat in the other, feeling very happy. We had a lot of cocoa to drink, brought the *Ran Muthu* back to the spot, anchored over it, and prepared to raise the cannon.

This time, I went down with an aqualung, and managed to maneuver the cannon over a very tricky ledge. After that, we tied two thick ropes on it, and after a great deal of heaving and hauling and pulling, we at last got the cannon onto the boat. We felt quite relieved and happy and for the next hour or two were banging away at the cannon and cleaning it.

We spent a lot of time, in the next few days, breaking off the coral which formed a rocky crust over almost the entire surface of the cannon. The best way of getting rid of this was by straight, hard bangs with a small hammer—being careful to hit only the coral, not the metal of the gun. Eventually the white lime would break up into powder and flake away; beneath it, the gun was in almost perfect condition, showing no signs of corrosion or wear. It was hard to believe that it came from the same ship as the badly worn swivel guns that Mike had recovered on the earlier expedition.

Though we searched carefully, we found no crests, insignia, or other markings on the cannon which would tell us anything about its ownership. But we did discover, stamped around the breech, a series of numbers: 2 3 23 8. They proved that the gun was of European origin, and we hoped —rightly, as it turned out later—that they would tell an expert a great deal more than that.

Rodney and I spent a great deal of time making a plan of the cannon, with all its dimensions. At first sight, this looked a simple job, but it proved to be nothing of the sort. A cannon is really an extremely complicated object, owing to its numerous bands, changes of diameter, trunnions, and cascabel (the knob at the end of the breech). The sometimes almost unbearable heat of the shed did not help us; I had made over fifty measurements, and had still not pinned down all the dimensions of the cannon, when I decided to call a halt through sheer exhaustion.

It had been a good day's work, marred only by three minor disasters. In addition to the van, *both* underwater movie cameras were out of action—one probably for good. It had flooded on the first dive and was half full of water; when we unloaded the soggy mess hours later, the battery-driven motor was still running feebly. (I will be glad to give the manufacturers a testimonial.) The other camera was not damaged, but its finder had been so bent that the operator could not tell what he was photographing. In the ordinary way, we would have been quite upset by these accidents, but we realized that they were a small price to pay for what we had won from the sea. If we felt depressed, we had only to look at the beautiful cannon lying on the floor of the shed—or think of the silver tucked away inside *Ran Muthu*.

Not to mention the much larger amount still waiting, we were now sure, out there in that valley on the reef.

20

Recipe for an

Underwater Archaeologist

It may seem odd that, with a fortune in silver lying there to be dug up, Mike and Peter spent at least half their diving time making maps and collecting old bronze cannons, wooden pistol stocks, rusty hand grenades and similar items of no commercial value. But we were determined to act like scientists, not looters, and we wanted to learn everything that we could about this wreck. It was, after all, the first treasure ship ever found in the Indian Ocean, and it was our responsibility to see that the secrets it carried were not lost.

Moreover, there was a good practical reason for our behavior. If we could identify the ship, there was an excellent chance that we could discover her cargo. The Dutch and British merchants who were operating in this area at the beginning of the eighteenth century kept careful records of all their shipments, and most of these documents still exist in the various national archives, where skilled research workers can dig them out. A complete listing of this wreck's cargo, besides being of great interest, would be extremely valuable to us. It

151

would tell us what to look for, and perhaps even *where*, if
Peter was able to work out the plan of the ship.

This would not be easy, and in one of our evening recording sessions down on the quiet beach he outlined the problems of underwater archaeology in general, and this site in
particular—

Peter:

This business of working on wrecks is not a game, it's
not a pleasant sport for Sunday divers. It's a tough, dirty
job which can only be done by trained, disciplined
crews, who are led by somebody who knows just what
he's doing. Whether they're professionals or amateurs
doesn't matter; the amateurs are usually better than professionals because you need guys who are pretty intelligent, and can see what something is before they smash
it on the bottom, and so forth.

And again, you've got to distinguish between archaeology and salvage. What we're doing now isn't archaeology, although I suppose what we're doing with the
material once we record it is archaeology. We're sal-
vaging stuff from this site, we're not recording it properly. The question of responsibility is entirely mine, and
it seems to me a logical and acceptable decision, because
it's quite obvious to me, and I believe I can prove this by
the photographs we've taken, by the way the material's
come up, by notes, that nothing we're finding is in context. We're not finding stuff that simply fell down from
a ship that sank, and that gradually fell apart. We're
getting stuff that's been washed into a big crevice in a
reef, and fallen down as this ship smashed. And I mean,
cannon balls and pistols and bags of silver and bits of
splintered planking and the squares of ship nails that
have disappeared completely as the iron has rotted away,
does not indicate that this material means very much

whether something came from one foot to one side or two feet to another side.

Again, we've got the problem of the monsoon. We've got this wreck, the materials, and they are not all necessarily important. For instance, today I raised a pistol. Well, the pistol stock is intact—it's very hard wood, not rotted at all—it's hardly been affected. The iron in the barrel and lock of the pistol has disappeared almost completely, and I exposed the thing, found the flintlock of the pistol. It would have been possible, at the expense of four or five dives, to have cut out the whole block and brought the pistol ashore in order to save the flintlock part of the pistol, which was, as I said, rusted away completely. Again, what's the use? We all know what flintlock pistols look like; the museums of the world are packed away with flintlock pistols of this kind. The stock of a pistol is probably sufficient for identifying the pistol and who made it and where, and all we're going to establish from the very rusted and fragile bits of iron is that it was a flintlock, and it obviously *had* to be a flintlock in 1700. So what's the use of saving the rusted lock?

Again, we're dealing with large quantities of money, and it's obviously more important to raise this stuff and get it out of there than to make a lot of plans which can't be made very well anyway because of the surge and which won't prove anything anyway beyond the obvious fact that the whole thing is a smashed-up mess, and then risk somebody else coming along and raising it. What can be raised easily this year, we should raise. It would still be desirable to make a plan of this wreck, to put down a drafting frame to make a very careful plan. I think that this is one of the very few circumstances in my career that I've ever seen a wreck that I thought it was legitimate to work on without making a plan. The reason we can't make a plan right now, of course, is the problem of the surge, the problem of personnel; but basically it's the problem of the surge in this place. Today the waves were breaking about ten feet high. The big ones were about fifteen feet high. We had a man—our sailor, Laza, who is a very good sailor and good seaman, and whom I find it a great pleasure to work with—and he kept the rubber dinghy more or less over us; and when he saw a big wave coming, he'd row thirty or forty feet out to sea so that the wave didn't break over the dinghy. . . .

If you didn't wedge yourself very carefully into the rock, getting your feet on the rock on one side and holding onto something with your hands and sort of holding yourself with all four members of your body, you were whipped right around and washed ten feet in either direction as the waves broke; and when a particularly big wave broke, you were often washed loose anyway, and had to clutch frantically for a handhold to keep from being swept twenty or thirty feet away. So it was a very hard job to work with a sledge hammer while lying flat on the bottom, hoping the current didn't wash you out of position or bang you against the coral and injure you.

Now I was very glad for the boiler suit that Mike had thoughtfully provided for me to wear. Its knees are almost worn out.

What we're planning now is, to go on, go to work, work like mad and see if there is really a lot more material in this cleft in the rock to make it worth while to go back to the wreck and work again. We're also going to carefully measure each of the cannons.

By the way, we'd originally estimated that there were ten cannons on the wreck, and the latest count is that there are four cannons around the two anchors in the bow part of the wreck, there are two cannons in between the bow part of the wreck and the heap of cannons, and there are now fourteen cannons, we have decided, in the heap of cannons—two of which are long guns, the rest of which are cannonades. So what we thought was a ten-gun ship now turns out to be at least a twenty-two-gun ship, because the twenty guns actually on the wreck and the one gun over the reef, that is to the north of the wreck, which was probably on the poop when it broke loose, makes twenty-one. This is not a logical number for a ship—it should have been twenty-two, so we've got a twenty-two or twenty-four-gun ship as it seems to be quite likely that there are cannons left on the site that we haven't seen yet because everything is so thickly over-grown with sea growth that it's very difficult to see.

With all these guns, it's interesting that we've only found about three cannon balls and seven or eight hand grenades. It would be logical to expect the hand grenades to be where they are in the aft end of what's left of the ship, because they would have been in the powder room, stored in the powder room along with the other combustible materials. But all of the cannon balls in the ship must be somewhere, and where they are must be the bottom of the hold of the ship, and we haven't even found those yet, which just goes to show how far we are from even scratching the surface of this extremely inter-esting wreck of what now seems to be a much bigger and more important ship than we originally thought it was.

It's surprising we've not found any other artifacts from this wreck. We should have found things from the cap-tain's cabin—silver plates, spectacles, watches, more glassware. Again, this just goes to show that we're only dealing with the very bottom of the ship, and a very, very small part of it. Everything we've raised to date has come from a one metre square area.

As you will see, we eventually did discover a few everyday objects, but on the whole our finds contrasted remarkably with those from the only similar site I know—the wreck of

El Matanzero, off the coast of Yucatan. (See Clay Blair's *Diving for Treasure.*) *El Matanzero,* a heavily laden Spanish merchant vessel, sank in 1741 on a reef very similar to ours, though only a few hundred feet off shore. She was discovered in 1957 by Bob Marx, and we were fascinated by Clay Blair's often hilarious account of the attempts to salvage her cargo. In many ways our problems were identical; everything was smashed up and buried by coral, and the divers were hampered by a terrific surge on the reef. On the other hand, we did not have to cope with scores of would-be divers and hangers-on, or wrestle for months with a suspicious and inefficient bureaucracy for permission to get anything done.

More than twelve thousand items were recovered from the wreck of *El Matanzero*—mostly trade goods like devotional medals, crucifixes, buttons, spoons, buckles, knife handles, beads. In addition there were pipe stems, thimbles, pottery, a watch, eyeglasses, decanter stoppers—but no treasure.

We found practically nothing but treasure. Well, you can't have everything; the buttons and eyeglasses can wait. Indeed, for all I know there may be a whole collection of them at the back of my house right now, in the large lumps that Peter salvaged but never had time to crack.

Working with Peter, hearing his tales of adventures in many lands, and watching the conscientious way in which he tackled the problems we had dumped into his lap, we became very impressed with his competence and the quite extraordinary range of his talents. So one evening, at the end of his usual forty-eight-hour day, I pinned him in a corner, handed him the microphone, and said, "Peter—I want your autobiography." The result was one of the most fascinating and improbable histories I have ever encountered; here it is:

My name is Peter Throckmorton. I was born in New York City in 1928. I battered around the world with my parents, who were divorced when I was very small, and both married again, so I lived with both of them in various places. I was a rather difficult child when I was a small boy, and always had a thing about the sea and ships and sunken ships. I suppose I got interested—when I was about seven or eight—with the idea of sunken ships, and I have been interested ever since.

When I was sixteen, I ran away from school. I was a disaster; I was thrown out of lots of schools, and became a salvage diver, beginning at about eighteen or nineteen. I worked at it for about a year-and-a-half as a hard hat diver in the Pacific. Then I got hurt, and decided to get into the Navy. But I couldn't because I had bad eyes— and so I joined the Army, and I got involved in the Army Transportation Corps, running ships. It was a very interesting and useful experience, because when I was twenty-one, I was working in a big shipyard in Japan.

While I was in Japan in the Army—I was there for four years—I was a Japanese interpreter. I passed my Language Qualification Test, went to school to learn Japanese, and I spent my spare time studying anthropology. I was all the time either working in the shipyard, or working on harbor launches as the coxswain, or captain of small harbor launches. Eventually I was made corporal, and rose to the command of a sixty-five feet high-speed boat. This was during the Korean War.

I got out of the Service in 1951, and ended up in Honolulu, where I'd been working back in 1946. While I was in the Army, I'd passed my university admission qualification test, and done my two years of university work by correspondence course, so I got into the University of Hawaii as a student in anthropology, and in my spare time was involved in a fishing business.

We originally started buying salvaged stuff from the Army and Navy, that they'd left all over the South Pacific, and so I battered around from 1951 to 1955 going to university, studying anthropology, and working in this salvage business. We finally ended up with a couple of big fishing boats. The business was eventually a failure, but I made quite a lot of money out of it for a time. We did a lot of interesting things in that business—we ran fishing boats down to the Central Pacific, down to Christmas Island, deserted Central Pacific islands and out into the Western Pacific as far as Pearl and Hermes Reef and Wake Island.

I was, of course, involved in diving at that time. I got involved in 1951 with aqualung diving. Having been a hard hat diver, I was fascinated by the whole idea of the aqualung, and started a business called Underseas Hawaii. That was the first business in Hawaii to do with renting aqualungs and teaching people to dive. Among other things, we salvaged diesel engines from ships sunk down in the New Hebrides. We bought minesweepers and delivered them to South Pacific places—Indonesia, Tahiti, New Caledonia. We did a lot of crazy things like that. I once went to work for the French Government on contract and delivered a small landing barge, an L.C.T., from Honolulu to Tahiti. We bought ships all over the Pacific and sold them.

Well, finally, what happened to me, I suppose, I got involved in the office. If you're involved in a business you've got to work in the office, and I decided I'd rather be an anthropologist. So I sold out my share of this business, which was fairly prosperous, and I went back to school full time. I got a chance to go to the University of Mexico, Mexico City College, and went on with my anthropology. The thing I'd been interested in in anthropology was Pacific migration—how the Polynesians got where they are, and how people communicated by ships across the Pacific; and having sailed around the Pacific so much in small ships, I was studying something I knew something about. So I went to Mexico City, stayed there studying anthropology and archaeology, and then I went to the University of Paris, where I stayed for nearly two years.

Finally, my G.I. bill ran out, and I went to work as a journalist, and I worked as a photographer, until 1958. I'd quit diving because I thought, well, it was a mug's game as far as I was concerned. It was just a waste of time. It was a nice sport, but it's a shame to sacrifice your life for a nice sport.

In the two years that I was full time professionally involved in journalism, I did a lot of stories, and I went all over the world, mostly photographing,[1] and writing about expeditions, things that had to do with my old interest of anthropology. I stayed with primitive people in various places in India, Assam, then in North Africa.

Eventually, I ended up in South Turkey, on a story for a magazine, and in a village down there I was introduced to some sponge divers. I was, of course, fascinated by this, because of my old interest in diving, and I asked if I could go on a trip with them. So I did go on a trip with some of the sponge divers I met, and I found that they knew about quantities of ancient shipwrecks under the ocean. I spent the next two years—in two summers, six or seven months—living with the Turkish sponge divers on their sponge boats, and diving with them, diving for sponges to pay for my keep, and took one dive a day to look at an ancient wreck which they'd show me. I became great friends with a captain there, who showed me all sorts of ships.

---

[1] Though he doesn't mention this, I suspect that Peter is the only magazine photographer who has stunned a machine-gun-carrying soldier, using his Leica as a weapon. He performed this act—far beyond the normal call of journalistic duty—in defense of his precious negatives, while purporting to hand them over. To keep Peter out of trouble, I won't mention the nationality of the soldier; your first guess will probably be wrong.

And my explorations—really, I'd been trained as an anthropologist and as an archaeologist, as an anthropology archaeologist, not a classical archaeologist; but I'd worked on excavations whenever I'd had the chance. The first excavation I worked on was in 1948 in Japan, digging neolithic pit-dwellings. I'd just spent all my leaves in Japan working as an assistant at the Archaeological Institute outside Tokyo. I'd learned to dive in 1946, and being both somewhat of a diver and somewhat of an anthropology archaeologist—well, not very qualified in either field—I'd had ideas about how an underwater excavation could happen, and I wondered why good underwater excavations had never been done.

So finally, in 1960, I became involved, and I've been involved ever since, with the University of Pennsylvania Museum and Dr. George Bass, who is a trained classical archaeologist with an M.A. from Johns Hopkins and a doctorate from the University of Pennsylvania. George Bass and I went out to do what is probably the first really scientific underwater excavation in history, which is the wreck of a Mycean ship which sank about 1200 B.C. off Cape Gelidonya, South Turkey. This was quite a successful excavation—we did manage to do it properly and make plans and it's going to be a very important archaeological publication. There have been many publications and papers about it, mostly by Bass, but some by me, and Bass and me together.

Since that time I've been associated with the University of Pennsylvania Museum. Like George Bass, I'm a research associate of the University Museum, and I've been working in Greece. My job is surveying for ancient shipwrecks in the Aegean, which means that I live with and talk to sponge divers who find the wrecks, and what we're trying to do basically is underwater archaeology as a disciplined science. We're trying to convince people that underwater archaeology is possible. We have now got an underwater archaeology project at the University of Pennsylvania Museum, which is run by George Bass. George is now Special Assistant for Underwater Archaeology, and has been excavating a Byzantine period ship of the time of Heraclius, which sank about 620 A.D. I also discovered this, again near Bodrum, which is our base in South Turkey. This is a very interesting wreck. It's a complete ship almost under the mud. The whole bottom section of the ship is complete.

Last summer, I surveyed two wrecks in Greece, both in shallow water. One was carrying a cargo of sarcophagi and the other one a cargo of columns. The column wreck looks about 500 A.D. and the sarcophagi about 300 A.D., both carrying material from Egypt.

What else can I say about myself? I speak Greek and Turkish, and know several other languages—used to know Japanese. I've written several—a good many—articles about underwater archaeology; the most spectacular ones have come out in the *National Geographic*. I'm now just finishing a book about my work in Turkey with the University Museum in 1958, '59 and '60. It's called *The Lost Ships*. It will be brought out by Atlantic Monthly Press next year. And I'm in the middle of another book about the history of underwater archaeology as a science, underwater archaeology in the Mediterranean.

So now you know the recipe for an underwater archaeologist. Stir well, allow to simmer—and stand well back.

21

Piranhas

and Elephants

The day after the bronze cannon was recovered, we ran into more bad luck. Perhaps I was the Jonah, for I had decided to come out to the reef and watch operations again.

It was a lovely, calm morning, perfect for diving; but we had sailed only two miles from Kirinda before one of the engines stopped. Apparently it had overheated, and we suspected that the hot gases still leaking from the faulty plumbing of the exhaust system were responsible. This problem, which had plagued us for the entire trip, had not arisen on any of *Ran Muthu's* shake-down cruises, but it practically wrecked our expedition and cut our diving time to a mere fraction of what it should have been. Even worse, the struggle with the balky, smoking engines and left Mike nauseated and exhausted, quite unable to work efficiently underwater—still less to do much of the filming we had planned.

So we returned to Kirinda, ripped out the broken exhaust piping, and sat around looking gloomily at the horrid mess of carbonized metal. There was nothing for it, Mike decided, but to drive back to Colombo with the bits and pieces, and get an entire new system built. He left at dusk with Hector, the two of them proposing to take turns at driving through the night. The rest of us would stay holding the fort until the boat was repaired—which, even with the best of luck, would take at least three days.

Although it was maddening to think of the opportunities we were missing, our enforced vacation had its advantages. It allowed Mike and Peter to recuperate from their diving exertions, and there was plenty to do on land—checking equipment, making notes, photographing the finds. Every so often we would go down to the beach and look thoughtfully at the waves, wondering how long the sea would remain calm, and how much time we would have left, even if we could get *Ran Muthu* working properly again.

Our unwanted holiday also gave us a chance of sampling some of the forgotten amenities of civilization. I have already mentioned the small town of Tissamaharama; it is only six miles from Kirinda and boasts what is possibly the finest rest-house in Ceylon. One of the Government Tourist Bureau's showplaces, it is up to the standards of most Western motels, and it is beautifully situated on the shore of a great artificial lake, several miles across. The dry zone of Ceylon is dotted with such lakes, part of an irrigation system two thousand years old yet still fulfilling the plans of its designers—the finest hydraulic engineers that the ancient world ever produced.

When we arrived at the great bund holding back the waters of Tissamaharama Lake, we found that Rodney, who had gone ahead of us, was taking a dip in the shallows. He was surrounded by thousands of fish (Blackspots) which had gathered at the lake's edge, expecting to be fed by the stale crusts that enterprising small boys sold to passersby.

I bought a loaf, tore off a piece, and threw it into the lake. The reaction was incredible—the water seemed to explode.

At once all the fish for yards around converged upon the spot, until the surface of the lake was a solid mass of bodies, twinkling and flashing in the sun. It was literally impossible to see the water for fish; they were as tightly packed as in a trawler's net when it is drawn aboard. Many of the fish in the center were forced up into the air by their companions, as they jostled frantically together.

We could make the school move anywhere we pleased, by throwing bread in different directions. I was particularly interested to note that the fish started to move toward the impact area while the food was still in flight; they obviously had excellent vision and good target-prediction computers.

Peter was photographing the boiling, heaving mass when we realized that some human interest would give him a much better picture. So we started dropping our crusts around Rodney, who was soon standing waist deep, not in water, but in Blackspots. As Rodney sank beneath the surface, shrieking and waving his arms realistically, Peter was able to get a gruesomely convincing series of photographs. (Not all Rodney's shrieks were feigned; Blackspots can nip.) If you ever see an illustrated article by P. Throckmorton in one of the tough men's magazines, describing how he lost a companion in the Upper Amazon (while his camera was providentially handy), you will know exactly how it was done.

Leaving Rodney slapping on Band-Aids, we drove to the resthouse, booked a room, and took turns having showers to wash away the accumulated brine of our diving operations. (Fresh water was in short supply at Kirinda beach; the well was several hundred yards away, and every drop had to be carried to the lighthouse shed in buckets.) Then we sat on the veranda and admired the lake's chief attraction—a small island, just in front of the resthouse, that has been turned into a bird sanctuary.

One could hardly see the trees for herons, storks, flamingos, and egrets, which were nesting on the island in countless thousands. Even though I have never been addicted to bird-watching, I was quite happy to spend an hour or so sweeping the sanctuary with my Questar, which brought it so close that I could see every detail of every feather, and could intrude upon many avian disagreements and domestic upheavals.

Tissamaharama must be an ornithologist's paradise, but still more interesting is the great game reserve of Yala twenty miles to the east. We took Peter there that same afternoon, to give him a rest from chipping coral at Kirinda.

Yala is some two hundred square miles of territory in the dry zone, where all hunting is forbidden. Visitors are welcome, but they must stay in their cars and be accompanied by an official guide. After we had filled in the necessary forms and collected our guide at the entrance to the sanctuary, we drove slowly for fifteen miles through narrow jungle roads, keeping our cameras at the ready. We never knew what we would see around the next corner, and there was one slightly anxious moment when we found a big bull elephant converging upon us. Though elephants usually ignore cars, we did not stop to test this one's reactions, but stepped on the accelerator.

A little later we overtook a large black object shambling down the road ahead of us with a most peculiar gait; it was a bear, obviously more at home in the trees than on ground level. We also met boar, deer (one group forming a beautiful frieze against the edge of a lake, as the sun went down behind them), and peacocks. We saw no leopards, but they probably saw us.

The most attractive sight was a solitary elephant, browsing in a forest glade. She looked so peaceful that I wished we could walk up and make friends, but this would not have been a good idea. Only a few years ago a rash movie photographer left the safety of his car in search of a better camera angle; I am told that the last footage he ever shot is quite exciting, though not too well focused.

Mike and Hector arrived from Colombo the next morning, with a new set of exhaust pipes—but it took us two days to fit them, as they had not been properly matched to the engines. It was a filthy, nauseating job working aboard *Ran Muthu* as she tossed and bucked at anchor out in the bay; sometimes I would glance through the telescope to check progress, then turn hastily away at the sight of the repair crew, heaving feebly on deck. But at last the installation was complete; we were (touch wood) operational again.

Unfortunately, the hold-up over the faulty exhaust system had not only cost us four days of diving; it had also cost us Rodney, who had to leave under contract to survey the intake housing for the turbines at Castlereagh Dam. (See Chapter 2.) His departure left us critically short of divers and threw a still heavier burden on Mike and Peter; but at least he left his splendid icebox behind.

When *Ran Muthu* finally set out again after her brief holiday, I remained on shore. The sea had been getting rougher during the last few days, and sometimes great waves would hit the rocky headland to the west of Kirinda and send curtains of spray shooting up into the air. This was not at all promising, and I feared that I had made my first and last visit to the reef this season.

While I was waiting for the boat to return, I persuaded some of the local youngsters to record their village songs, and the playbacks caused endless amusement (Fig. 7). Having established a fund of good will with the tape recorder, I had no difficulty in getting volunteers to carry telescope, tripod, and cameras up to the top of the hill overlooking Kirinda. They were fascinated to see the lighthouse and passing ships brought from ten miles to within a few hundred yards, but I was much more interested in *Ran Muthu,* as she bobbed up and down on the far side of the reef.

Visibility was remarkably good, despite the ten miles of hot, trembling air that lay between my hilltop and the Great

Basses. So I coupled the Nikon to the Questar, held a large red filter from an aerial surveying camera over the objective, and shot off a roll of film. When I developed it back in Colombo, I was quite pleased with the result; *Ran Muthu's* canvas awning was clearly visible, peeping above the breakers foaming over the reef, with the white tower of the lighthouse looming in the background.

I watched from the hill for over an hour, swinging the telescope around the sky from time to time to look at the ships that were steaming past this busy crossroads in the sea. Then, when I saw that *Ran Muthu* was bound for home I went back to the lifeboat shed and told Anthony to get tea ready for the hungry divers.

Mike and Peter had spent most of the day learning more about the complicated geography of the wreck, and had made some interesting discoveries. Peter had found a cannon no less than ten feet long; all the rest, except for our bronze one, were eight-footers. Mike had located a whole pile of ballast stones, and had also discovered a fine copper serving plate, about eighteen inches in diameter, cemented into a mass of cannon balls and small chunks of coins. He worked for a long time to chip this plate loose, but did not succeed.

He also found a bronze pestle, in perfect condition, and spent some time looking for the mortar to go with it. But Mike never succeeded in completing the set; the mortar is still somewhere out there on the reef.

It was on this dive that Mike had his narrowest escape of the whole expedition, though he did not realize it until some hours later. He lost his hold in a sudden surge, and was swept about twenty feet upward toward the surface. The abrupt and unexpected drop in pressure apparently strained his lungs, for that night he had a severe pain in his chest. We were all very worried, but fortunately by next morning he was completely fit. If he had been swept upward a little more rapidly, or had tried to hold his breath while the pressure around him suddenly dropped, he might well have been killed.

It was a clear warning for all of us; and yet, the very next morning, and on the spur of the moment, I decided to ignore it.

22

Caught

in the Surge

Ran *Muthu* left late on the morning of April 21; though the exhausts had, at long last, been fixed, the fuel supply to one engine had failed. (That all these setbacks might not be accidental did not—perhaps luckily—occur to us until a good deal later.) By adapting one of the outboard motor fuel tanks, Mike managed to jury-rig an emergency supply.

I had had no intention of going on this trip; my one dive, I felt, had been tempting Providence far enough. But just before the boat was leaving, Mike suddenly remarked: "Why don't you come?" I heard a voice, which must have been my own, reply "O.K."—and before I knew what had happened I was splashing through the surf into the rubber dinghy.

We climbed aboard *Ran Muthu*, only to find that the engine with the temporary fuel-feed would not turn over. It had seized up completely, and though Mike tore off the hatches and worked on it like a demon, there was nothing that he could do. I sat on the foredeck, very disappointed yet perhaps secretly relieved, waiting for the order to reload the dinghies and return to land.

It did not come. To my astonishment and alarm, Mike announced that we would go out on one engine. I felt that I should put my foot down, and veto this suggestion; after all, the whole idea of having two engines in *Ran Muthu* had been to give us a margin of safety on the reef. If one engine had failed mysteriously, could we rely on the other?

I protested, but no one took any notice. Even Peter, whom I had expected to give me some moral support, seemed quite unconcerned. I could put on flippers and swim back to land (I'd done it once before, just to prove that I could), but that fear of making an excessive fuss which is responsible for most acts of heroism stopped me. Full of forebodings, I watched the mainland recede, and waited for our one engine to stop at any moment. What Mike had planned to do if this happened, I still have no idea; but I now suspect that by this time he was thinking of ways of collecting *Ran Muthu's* insurance.

We got to the reef without incident and dropped anchor at our usual position, a hundred yards on the seaward side of the wreck. Soon after we had arrived, when I was conversing with Mike and Peter, I was startled by a big manta jumping right into my field of vision, only fifty feet from the boat; it fell back with a crash before anyone else could turn to look at it. Though they are common enough, it was the first time that I had seen one of these strange beasts in Ceylon waters.

Conditions looked quite good, so I had no hesitation in putting on a single tank aqualung and climbing—or rather falling—into the dinghy with Mike and Peter. Laza rowed us across to his usual parking site fifty feet from the wreck, and we rolled into the water.

I submerged very slowly, to give my ears plenty of time to adjust. (Eight years earlier, on the Great Barrier Reef, I had punctured an eardrum and have been very careful ever since.) Mike, who was keeping an eye on me, got the impression that I was not carrying enough weight to sink properly; so he swam over and handed me the four pound hammer that he had been using to chip away the coral.

This took me down rather too fast, and I was so busy trying to blow my nose and clear my ears that I did not notice that the current was carrying me toward the reef. For suddenly, without any warning, I was seized by an irresistible force; I was absolutely helpless, as if in the grip of a giant hand.

The surge was swinging me back and forth—first toward the jagged, barnacled rocks of the reef, then away from them. Between each reversal of the current, there were a few seconds while I hung motionless and had a chance to think; then I would be grabbed again as the hundreds of tons of water started moving once more. I was trapped, like a fly in amber, in the heart of an invisible, liquid pendulum.

Only a few yards away, I could see the wall of the reef rising like a cliff; its highest levels, just below the rocking, mirror surface of the water, were almost hidden in a white mist of foaming bubbles—as the peaks of a mountain range may be shrouded by clouds. My great fear was that I would be swept up toward those peaks, and over them into the the seething water on top of the reef. Even a diver in good health would be badly knocked about—if nothing more—as he went over those rocks; in my condition, I was pretty sure I would have no chance of survival.

I was almost equally worried about my aqualung mouthpiece, for it seemed that at any moment the surge would tear it from my teeth. I had to use my left hand to hold it in place —while my right was still frozen firmly onto the hammer that was inexorably pulling me down.

Unfortunately, it was not pulling me down fast enough. I had hoped to descend into deeper, calmer water, but it was obvious that I was being dragged too swiftly toward the upper slopes of the reef. Now those deadly rocks, with their covering of razor-sharp barnacles, were only inches away, and I was smashing straight toward them.

There was only one thing to do, and I did it quite instinctively. I held out the hammer, and let it take the shock of the impact. Then the pendulum swing of the surge swept me away again.

A second time I crashed against the rocks, still more violently. It was then—a little late, you may think—that I began to realize the seriousness of the situation. But I determined not to panic, for I knew that would be fatal. About three years earlier, I had been caught in heavy surf off one of the Ceylon beaches and pounded down by the waves; Mike had got me out, at great risk to himself, with only seconds to spare. On that occasion I had felt the horrible, numbing fear that can drain all the strength from a man's limbs, and all the reasoning power from his brain, turning him instantly into a terrified and helpless animal.

Holding out that hammer as a buffer, I fought simultaneously against the surge, and against panic. I do not know how many more times the iron head of the hammer clanged against the reef; probably no more than two or three. Then I realized that my only hope lay in dropping the hammer, which was immobilizing my one good arm, turning away from the reef, and swimming with all my strength out to sea.

I waited until I was at the greatest distance from the rocks, then released the hammer and swam for my life with hands and flippers. Luckily, the dinghy was only a short distance away—it, too, seemed to have been dragged toward the reef —and I was able to reach it without difficulty. I clung thankfully to the trailing ropes, switched from aqualung to snorkel, and told Laza to tow me back to *Ran Muthu* as quickly as he could. I was not strong enough to climb into the dinghy, and did not want to waste time taking off the aqualung in the water.

I was slightly, but only slightly, worried at leaving Mike and Peter, but they had seen me reach the safety of the dinghy and when I last glimpsed them they were already settling down to work, as if these conditions were perfectly normal. When Laza rowed me away, I did have a sudden spasm of guilt; but it was definitely not because I was abandoning my colleagues to the mercy of the reef. I was worried in case I had lost the hammer, which was one of their most vital tools.

It seemed to take ages to get back to the boat, though I did my best to add a little speed with my flippers. The current toward the reef was obviously far stronger than it had been on any previous occasion; if it became any more powerful, I wondered if the divers would be able to make it back to *Ran Muthu*. I decided that, when the dinghy returned to the reef, it would be at the end of a long nylon rope; then, whatever the strength of the current, we would be able to haul everyone back to the boat. Unless, of course, our own anchor dragged.

With Laza pushing and Martin pulling, I scrambled back aboard *Ran Muthu*, gouging a small valley in my shin in the process. As so often happens with wounds received in the sea, I felt nothing at the time; but it remained an open sore which refused to heal for weeks.

We tied the nylon line to the dinghy, and sent Laza hurrying back to the reef while we played it out, making sure that there was no slack to get fouled in our propellers. All this seemed to take a very long time, and I began to get worried about Mike and Peter. Suppose, after all, they were in trouble?

To my vast relief, I saw Mike surface just as the dinghy arrived off the reef, and have a brief consultation with Laza. Then he went down again; obviously everything was under control.

I lay on the deck, slowly getting back my wind and my nerve, and wondering how the divers were faring. For the first time, I had shared their difficulties, and my already considerable admiration for them went up several points. Yet at the same time, I felt a little angry with them for getting me into such a dangerous situation in my semi-invalid state. They were aware of my limitations, so why had they let me dive?

It is easy to be wise after the event; I did not know, until we discussed the matter later, that the power of the current had been almost as big a surprise to them as it was to me. But they had the strength—and the hard won experience—to cope with it.

After two hours, while Laza bobbed around at the end of the line, occasionally paddling briskly away from the reef when a big roller came along, Mike and Peter surfaced and climbed into the dinghy. When they got back to the boat, they had with them some small sacks of loose coins—and the fine copper tray or plate that Mike had been chipping away at for two days (Fig. 53). Beneath its coral coating, it was in excellent condition, apart from a few cracks that Mike had made as he levered it out of the reef.

After the usual biscuits and hot cocoa, the divers returned to the wreck. They thought my nylon line was a good idea, but modified it by fastening a float at its middle so that it would not sink down and get tangled round the rocks on the seabed. So once again we had Laza bobbing at the end of two hundred feet of nylon, a small satellite of *Ran Muthu*.

By this time, I had completely recovered from the morning's fright, and felt curiously full of energy. Probably it was some kind of psychological reaction, and perhaps I felt a little ashamed of myself for my precipitate retreat. But I was sure that I had done the right thing; my motto all along had been: "Take risks if you *must*—but don't take unnecessary ones." Of course, it was sometimes very hard to know where to draw the line.

I tossed a few pieces of paper overboard, and noted that

they drifted away very slowly. The current had obviously slackened a good deal; by this time, conditions over at the reef would be much better.

It is said that the best thing to do with an airman who has just crashed is to send him up again at once; otherwise he may lose his nerve completely. I thought it over for a while, and then decided to put this theory into practice.

23

The Last Dive

There was no danger, the way I planned it. I put on face mask, flippers, weight belt—but no aqualung—gripped the snorkel in my teeth, and dropped over the side. Holding on to the nylon line with one hand, I swam and pulled myself slowly across to the dinghy. The trip was perfectly comfortable, and perfectly safe, even though I was alone in the treacherous waters of the Great Basses.

The nylon line, about as thick as my little finger, had a breaking strain of many hundreds of pounds, and was securely fastened to *Ran Muthu*. She in turn was held in place by twin anchors, so I felt completely confident as I worked my way over to the dinghy. Even though the current now seemed negligible, I took no chances. I never let go of the line, but either gripped it or kept one arm hooked affectionately around it.

The afternoon had become cloudy, and with the dimming of the sun the underwater view had become rather dull. There were no beautiful coral formations beneath me and not many fish. It was a drab no-man's-land of barnacled rocks and occasional pits and canyons.

Taking my time, I presently reached the dinghy and hovered underneath it—still holding on to the rope. Once again I peered down into that debris-filled little valley, whose secrets we had scarcely scratched. Mike was hammering away at the base of a small cliff, not far from the spot where the bronze cannon had rested for two and a half centuries. With this conspicuous signpost removed, the area was now just another uninteresting piece of seabed. The scar of the underwater operation had already been filled by loose coral, swept into it by the restless currents—which had even torn away some of the metal tags Peter had wired down as reference points for his map.

But where *was* Peter? I looked in all directions, up and down the valleys that stretched away into the distance. There was not the slightest sign of him; I could not even glimpse the regular bursts of silver bubbles which betray the presence of an aqualung diver. I was surprised, but not particularly worried, for Mike was digging away with happy unconcern and presumably knew where Peter had gone.

Amateur and sports divers are always told to practice the "buddy" system—to remain in sight of each other, and never to dive alone. This is excellent advice, and should be obeyed. But not by professionals, who may sometimes have to break the rules to do a job of work. I was sure that Mike and Peter, with their thousands of hours of underwater experience, knew exactly what they were doing.

After hovering above Mike for about ten minutes, still clinging to the rubber boat, I became more adventurous. There was fifty feet of extra nylon rope on the dinghy, and I lashed one end around my waist, coiled up the remainder in a few convenient loops, and cut adrift from my little floating island. I could now go swimming off in any direction, quite confident that I could pull myself back to the dinghy whenever I wished.

Mike was at a depth of about thirty feet, and I made several attempts to dive down to him. As might be expected, even my best efforts were pretty feeble; I was able to manage only about half the distance before having to turn back.

As I passed the bottom of each dive, I hooted and shouted into the water, but Mike took not the slightest notice. I gave up trying to attract his attention, and relaxed on the surface, watching his activities.

Presently, he dropped the hammer and crowbar he had been using, and started to swim away down the valley in a very purposeful manner. I guessed at once that he had found something interesting, and was going to find Peter. Unreeling my safety line, I swam immediately above him (he still hadn't noticed me), and was not at all surprised when, at last, I saw a cloud of white bubbles ahead with the dim shape of Peter under them.

The two divers swam back to Mike's little corner of the reef, and there was an excited consultation on the seabed. Then Peter came up to the dinghy and said: "Let me have a sack—Mike's found a couple of lumps as big as your head."

In the next five minutes, I had a perfect bird's-eye-view of the salvage operation, and I blessed my lucky stars that, despite the morning's scare, I had plucked up enough courage to come out to the reef again. For I was watching something which, I suppose, not more than a handful of living men have seen—the lifting of treasure from the seabed, at the actual moment of discovery.

The sack that Peter had taken down had been tied on to the end of my nylon line and was now resting on the coral. From time to time I gave it a tug; at first I was able to jerk it off the seabed, but it became steadily heavier as work progressed. Before long I was barely able to budge it, and I decided to get closer to the scene of operations.

It is very much easier to pull yourself down into the sea, going hand over hand along a fixed line, than it is to swim. Every diver knows this, and makes good use of convenient anchor chains as stairways. So this time I was able to get down to within a couple of yards of Mike and Peter; even when I had hauled myself down the line, I had used so little energy and air that I was able to hover effortlessly over the seabed for what seemed enormous periods of time. (They probably did not exceed thirty seconds—but you can see and do a great deal in half a minute.) I remember thinking that I was probably the first diver in history who had used solid silver ballast to pull himself down to the seabed.

Each time I dived, I descended a little further, and I would have touched bottom if the digging hadn't finished about then. It gave me a great feeling of satisfaction to know that I had come nearer to the wreck by my own lung power (which twelve months earlier had been practically zero) than I had ever been able to do with an aqualung.

Peter and Mike got this consignment of silver free from the reef with the last few breaths of air in their tanks. While they lifted it into the dinghy, I swam back ahead to alert Pieris, our photographer. We had intended to re-enact the recovery of the treasury, hauling some of the earlier lumps aboard *Ran Muthu* in front of the movie camera, but now there was no need for even this mild piece of cinematic faking. We were able to film the real thing, at the very moment it was happening.

We lay on the deck in the late afternoon sun, tired but very happy. Though no one said so in as many words, we all knew that the expedition was over, and it could hardly have ended on a better note. The Great Basses Reef, in a moment of mellow relaxation, had given us a parting gift—and it would be as well to take the hint. In any case, the advancing season, and our mechanical troubles, gave us no choice.

The two anchors came up for the last time, the single engine started (to my great relief) and we slowly drew out to sea. Mike did not take the shortest way back to Kirinda, even though it was getting late. Instead, he took a swing round the lighthouse, passing very close to it and going right over the scene of our earlier expeditions.

The water had now become almost uncannily still; there

was an oily calm, as if the reef was putting on its best behavior just to show what it could do when it felt like it. Beneath us I could see, wavering in the crystalline depths, the
drowned caves and grottoes through which we had once
swum with Ali Baba and Sinbad and Aladdin. It was with a
sense of sadness that we remembered that they were no
longer there.

The great granite tower of the lighthouse loomed above
us, a tree of stone rooted so securely in rock that it had with-
stood the gales of almost a century. One of the lightkeepers
was sitting on the lower platform, watching us as we chugged
past—so close that we could have tossed a package across to
him. "Goodby!" we called. "We'll be back next year!" Then
we headed for Kirinda, ten miles away.

Halfway there, as I dozed on the foredeck, I was startled
by a sudden explosion just behind me. Mike was blazing
away with his Luger at a piece of floating wood; it was only
his way of blowing off steam, but I wished he'd warned me.
I was still very conscious of the fact that we were running
on one engine.

We had never been out quite so late as this, for we had
always been careful to return to our anchorage well before
nightfall. The entry into Kirinda is tricky, owing to dangerous reefs and rocks, and is not to be attempted after dark.
Ran Muthu was still several miles out; and ahead of us now
was one of the most spectacular sunsets I have ever seen.

Miles inland, the sky was overcast by the black clouds of a
heavy rainstorm. But its center was clear, and in this we
could see the misty mountains that bear the name of one of
Ceylon's most sacred places, the shrine of Kataragama. They
were perfectly framed by the surrounding clouds, and the
sun was going down behind them, painting them in such
mysterious golds and purples that it was hard to believe that
they were real. No theatrical designer could have contrived
a more splendid stage setting; we seemed to be looking

straight into the heart of Fairyland. And I found myself thinking, as the light slowly faded from the western sky, that the beauty ahead of us was no illusion, no mere trick of sun and cloud. It was real, and we were returning to it, with our cargo of hard-won treasure.

24

Winding Up

So ended, homeward bound over a smooth, calm sea, the greatest (and very nearly the last) adventure of my life.

We hit the beach at dusk, tired but happy, and started unloading everything from *Ran Muthu*. A shuttle service with the rubber dinghies brought back cameras, aqualungs, diving gear, and all the valuables from the boat—including the silver. Each lump was wrapped in sacking and then securely tied with rope, so that none of our volunteer helpers could open it, accidentally or otherwise. So much heavy gear was carried up the beach from the boat to the shed that the treasure, as we had hoped, passed quite unnoticed, and Peter stowed it under my camp bed.

For the rest of the evening, we tried to ignore those shapeless lumps, though we were all very much aware of their presence. That night, I slept immediately above two hundredweight of silver; not surprisingly, I dreamed that I was collecting coins that the waves had tossed up on the beach.

We started packing at dawn, and managed to get everything—including ourselves—into the Oxford (now repaired) and the Volkswagen (returned by the police, though still needed as Exhibit A in the forthcoming trial). *Ran Muthu* we left bobbing at anchor in Kirinda Bay, securely moored to two anchors by heavy chains, and with her cabin pad-locked. Our two boatmen, Martin and Laza, had been on continuous duty for weeks, and we felt that we could not leave them behind while the rest of us drove to Colombo. We proposed to send them back to Kirinda in a few days, with a mechanic to repair the balky engine, and as soon as that was fixed they could sail *Ran Muthu* home. Meanwhile, we were sure, she could look after herself.

This was a mistake, and it might have been a very expensive one.

We waved goodby to Kirinda, and drove uneventfully back to Colombo, stopping once or twice to show Peter some of the local sights. It seemed a pity to have come all the way from Greece and to have seen nothing of Ceylon except the seacoast, but he had to return to Athens almost at once, to make the arrangements for his next expedition.

The longest of our brief stops was at the walled town of Galle, Ceylon's chief seaport before the building of Colombo harbor in the nineteenth century. We walked on the ramparts of the old fort, looked down into the clear waters, and made plans for the future. Within a few hundred yards of us lay the wreck of the only *known* treasure ship to go down off Ceylon. This was the P. & O. mail-steamer *Malabar,* which was sunk in 1860 by a monsoon storm while actually inside the harbor. There was no loss of life, but the ship carried an extremely valuable cargo—including the suite of Lord Elgin, later Viceroy of India. According to Potter's *The Treasure Diver's Guide,* some $450,000 of silver pesos also went down with her, but at least half of this was raised soon afterwards. As the *Malabar* was ideally placed for salvage operations, it is most unlikely that the divers left anything worthwhile inside her; but it would still be interesting to have a look.

There is another connection between Galle and the submarine world which must now be completely forgotten, and it is well worth recalling. Just a century ago, the first (to my knowledge) underwater color pictures were made on the coral reef near the fort, by an enterprising artist named Baron Eugene de Ransonnet. He constructed a small diving bell, just big enough to hold the upper part of his body, and weighed down with seven hundredweight of lead. Sitting inside it with his sketchbook, the baron had himself lowered into the water, while air was supplied from a pump in an adjoining boat.

The resulting quite superb studies—almost photographically accurate—were published in *Sketches of Ceylon* (Vienna 1867), and are still well worth reproducing. As we stood on the ramparts overlooking the spot where the baron sketched the underwater scenery of Ceylon, I could not help thinking that today we could get a better view with face mask and snorkel than he could with half a ton of diving bell.

Though we were all exhausted, there was no rest for us when we got back to Colombo. Before Peter left, we had to photograph, classify, and preserve the material we had salvaged. Wooden and iron objects that have been submerged in salt water for many years crumble to pieces after a few weeks when exposed to air, unless special precautions are taken. Mendel Peterson had sent us detailed instructions for avoiding this calamity; since all underwater explorers should know how to preserve their finds, I give these useful hints in an Appendix. Before long our house was littered with witches' cauldrons in which cannon balls and pistol butts were slowly simmering.

One of my first acts on returning to Colombo was to weigh the accumulated silver. For the main lumps the figures, in pounds, were: 30, 29, 29, 29, 28, 27, 24, 20. Allowing for smaller lumps, loose coins (many corroded or partly covered with coral) and the material sent to the Smithsonian, the total weight of silver we had recovered on the two expeditions was about three hundred and fifty pounds. All this had come from very few hours of actual diving on an area of two

or three square yards; if *Ran Muthu* had behaved, and Mike
and Peter had not been such conscientious archaeologists, the
haul would undoubtedly have been much greater.

The night before Peter flew out of Ceylon, we worked
into the small hours taking close-ups of all the important
finds, so that he would have photographs from which he
could continue his researches. We also had consultations with
the director of the Colombo Museum, Dr. P. E. P. Deraniya-
gala (now retired), and the archaeological commissioner,
Dr. C. E. Godakumbure, and started making arrangements
for a permanent exhibition of the material. It is our hope
that, in years to come, visitors to the Colombo Museum will
be able to see the coins, the guns and the other artifacts from
the first treasure ship ever discovered in the Indian Ocean—
as well as the photographic record of their recovery.

We still knew nothing about the origin or nationality of
the ship, but soon after our return we did make one very
interesting discovery. It was the first definite piece of information we had found concerning the wreck, and it may be
quite misleading. But here it is:

I have mentioned that the bronze cannon was marked on
the breech with the series of numbers 2 3 23 8. When
we wrote to the Smithsonian and asked Mendel Peterson
what this could mean, he answered at once that it was the
English way of indicating the weight of a gun. The "2" would
be hundredweights, the "3" quarter-hundredweights, and the
"23" the odd pounds. The final "8" was probably the number
of the gun. Allowing for the fact that in the peculiar British
system of measures a hundredweight is 112 pounds, this
would mean that the gun weighed 331 pounds.

It is not every set of kitchen scales that goes up to 331
pounds and it was some time before we could test this theory.
But finally we located a heavy-duty weighing machine,
hauled the cannon into the Volkswagen and drove it round
to the Ceylon Institute of Scientific and Industrial Research.

When we had got the cannon on to the platform, we were delighted to find that it weighed 332 pounds; the few patches of coral were quite enough to account for the negligible discrepancy. And I was amused to find that the modern scientific establishment whose precision scales we were borrowing used exactly the same system as the cannon-founders of almost three centuries ago; it was calibrated in hundredweights, quarter-hundredweights, and pounds, so that my actual readings were 2 3 24, as against the cannon's engraved 2 3 23.

The British Empire bequeathed many good things to its ex-colonies; but its system of weights and measures is not among them.

The gun, then, was definitely English. However, this proved nothing at all. In the course of its career, a gun might serve on many ships, changing hands either by purchase or the fortunes of war. Nevertheless, we began to take more seriously the theory that the ship had belonged to the British, rather than the Dutch, East India Company, and initiated research in England as well as Holland.

Now the time had come to say goodby to Peter, who had to return to his diving operations in colder and less colorful seas. We saw him aboard the Athens-bound *Comet*, and said we hoped he'd be back next year. He promised to keep in touch—a promise that he more than fulfilled. Scarcely had he disappeared into the west, it seemed, before a blizzard of notes and memoranda came winging back to us—including Appendix A, his detailed report on the wreck. But as I write these words I have not heard from him for several weeks; he is now at the bottom of the Aegean, digging down into the centuries before Christ.

Meanwhile, back at Kirinda, our worries were not over. We had sent Martin, Laza, and a mechanic from the shipyard to repair *Ran Muthu*, and they telephoned alarming news. They had found the boat swinging on one anchor, the smaller of the two that we had left. The mooring could never have parted by accident; someone must have cut the heavy rope.

There had also been an attempt to remove one engine, though luckily it had not progressed very far. That would have been a virtually impossible feat even in calm weather, and the sea was now becoming quite rough. We were all enormously relieved when our little crew managed to get *Ran Muthu*, on her one operating engine, back along the coast to the sheltered harbor of Tangalle. They would be able to carry out repairs there—safe from the machinations of our unknown friends at Kirinda.

At Tangalle, when the seized-up engine was stripped down, a thick coating of tar was found in the cylinders. The diesel experts maintained that there was only one way in which it could have got there; someone must have put it in the fuel tank. If so, it was lucky for us that we had two engines and two fuel systems. The saboteur had not done his job properly.

We may never know the truth about this matter, but we have several theories. The sight of an empty, brand new twin-engined cabin cruiser at anchor may have been too great a temptation for local pirates. Perhaps they hoped to encourage her to run aground, so that they could loot the wreck, and steal the valuable engines. Or there may have been a deeper plot, aimed at keeping us away from the reef. If so, it came too late; we had already finished for the season.

Ran Muthu's last voyage under our flag was completely uneventful. The engine was repaired, she sailed quietly back to Colombo, and returned to the shipyard where she had been built. But by this time we had decided that seagoing cruisers were too expensive a hobby, and we sold her to a local shipping company. She was a sturdy little boat and her new owners had a bargain.

A few days later, the first winds of the southwest monsoon started gusting across the city, overturning trees, scattering leaves and branches in every direction. Rain fell in torrents; the roads over which we had driven back from Kirinda were feet deep under water—or even swept away. We—and *Ran Muthu*—had got back just in time. Our luck, though not all we might have wished for, could have been very much worse.

We regarded the weather with some satisfaction. We now believed that the reports of rival expeditions, which had caused us so much alarm, were nothing more than wild rumors or hopeful exaggerations. But even if there was some truth in them, it did not matter now—nor would it for another year.

It was easy to imagine conditions out on the reef. The breakers would be pounding against the base of the lighthouse, shooting clouds of spray far up the granite tower. Shark's Tooth Rock would be hidden beneath the foam boiling and seething around it; no boat could possibly get near the site of the wreck without being dashed to pieces.

If anyone had told me that we would be there again in six weeks, I would have said that he was mad.

25

"Via Vida"

We had barely recovered, physically and financially, from the expedition, and I had already written the first half of this book, when we had some unexpected visitors. A floating film studio, in the shape of a converted United States minesweeper, sailed into Colombo harbor.

She was the *Via Vida,* owned by Artie and Vida Wayne, who had been cruising round the world for the last two years making a series of adventure-travel movies. Aboard ship were their three children, Pam, Little, and Gary, and several of their friends, who starred in the movies and so led a globe-trotting existence which would make any other teenagers green with envy.

The Waynes, who are now high on our long list of favorite Americans, contacted us soon after their arrival, and were much impressed by the treasure. It was agreed that they should shoot some footage of Mike explaining how it had been found; so one night my house was converted into a film studio and the entire unit moved in on me. Though I enjoyed watching Mike being reduced to the humble role of actor, and being forced by perfectionist Artie Wayne to run through some shots six or seven times, I retired to bed long before the filming was over, and my dreams were interrupted at irregular intervals by the bang of the clapper-board. The unit staggered back blearily to the ship at 5.A.M., and not for the first time I was very happy that I was no longer directly involved in film making.

Via Vida sailed the next day—and we sailed with her. Artie and Vida had invited us to come with them on a trip around Ceylon, from Colombo to Trincomalee, with a little diving on the way if conditions were suitable. Although the southwest monsoon was blowing intermittently on our side of the island, the sea should be calm around Trincomalee, the scene of so many of our adventures on the east coast. The chance of seeing the Great Basses Reef again, in luxurious surroundings and with some one else doing all the worrying, was far too wonderful to miss.

Elizabeth, Mike, and I boarded the *Via Vida* in the evening, and she pulled out of Colombo harbor just after sunset. After little *Ran Muthu*, she seemed enormous, and it took me a couple of days to find my way around. Built at the very end of the war at a cost of some $2,600,000, *Via Vida* had been promptly mothballed, and when Artie and Vida had purchased her at a bargain price she was thus a brand-new, twenty-year-old ship, 180 feet long and weighing nearly a thousand tons, she is one of the two or three largest privately owned vessels in the world. I was particularly impressed to discover that it cost more merely to fill her fuel tanks than we had paid for *Ran Muthu*.

We lived, ate (and drank) like lords as we rounded the island; the automatic ice-cube dispenser was seldom idle. Under a magnificent full moon by night, and an almost cloudless sky by day, we sailed down the coast in a state of complete relaxation. For entertainment there were screenings of the excellent films Artie and Vida had already made, recorded music while sunbathing on deck, and hilarious tales of Artie's stage and radio career, with thumbnail sketches of the great and not-so-great of show business.

But the highlight of the trip—the most enjoyable sea voyage I have ever made—came on the beautiful morning when we sailed past the Great Basses Reef. Echo-sounder pinging anxiously, Captain Homer Sayto took us on the landward side of the reef, and brought us to within a quarter of a mile of the lighthouse. It was with a strange feeling, almost of unreality, that I looked again upon the site of all our struggles and adventures—so close, but already unapproachable.

Although *Via Vida* was plowing smoothly along across a sea which was surprisingly calm for the time of year, the breakers were already thundering over the reef. The waves were approaching it at an acute angle, not quite broadside-on, so that a wall of spray would suddenly shoot at a colossal speed right along the reef from east to west. Against this erupting curtain of white water, Shark's Tooth Rock would appear in silhouette, like a black notch. And sometimes, because the relative motion tricked the eye, it would appear that the wall of spray was motionless, and that it was Shark's Tooth Rock that was hurtling from west to east.

I took some photographs of Mike and Elizabeth, with the reef in the background; it was the first time that she had ever seen the place where her husband had been intermittently risking his neck for almost five years. As we sailed past the lighthouse, we flashed a message of good wishes to the staff on duty. They must have wondered what Mike Wilson was doing aboard a small battleship, for in her gray paint *Via Vida* still looked distinctly warlike—a fact that the Waynes had found of considerable advantage in some troubled waters.

An hour later, we were skirting the long ridge of the Little Basses, and its lighthouse was on the horizon. (Please do not ask me why the Little Basses Reef is considerably *larger* than the Great Basses Reef.) To all of us, this was unknown territory; how many ships, how much treasure, had been shared by this twenty-mile-long submarine trap? It is perhaps even deadlier than its twin, because it comes much closer to shore —and most old-time shipping tended to hug the coast.

We knew of one important ship that had come to grief

here, and I had the court-martial of her captain with me aboard *Via Vida*. Just past the Little Basses the charts show an obstruction labeled "Daedalus Rock"; this is how it got its name.

The *Daedalus* was a forty-gun frigate captured by the British from the French in 1811; she weighed 1,094 tons, had a length of 153 feet, and carried a crew of 274. Her career in the British Navy was a very brief one. Here is her captain's own account of how it ended. We find it particularly fascinating because it is the only eyewitness account of a grounding on the Basses; if there were any survivors from our own wreck a few miles to the southwest, they might well have told an almost identical story.

ADM 1/05437
> *Extracts from the* COURT MARTIAL *on*
> HMS "DAEDALUS" *on 11th August 1813*

Captain Murray Maxwell's Letter, 7th July 1813.

We sailed from Spithead with charge of the East India Convoy on the 29th of last January and made Point de Galle (Ceylon) at noon 1st July, passed Dondrehead at Sunset and then steered E by N during the Night to pass well outside the Basses which, soon after daylight, on the Morning of the 2nd by our course and distance both the Master and myself felt assured we had done and in consequence steered North to get in with the Land again, keeping a good look out both from the Deck and mast head for Rocks and Breakers; lest our distance should have been affected in the Night by any current, and as the morning was perfectly clear, and nothing whatever seen to indicate danger, when we got to what we conceived to be within seven or eight Miles of the land, and shaped our course along it, the Convoy closely following us, and from the cross bearing of the land marks, which

the Master pointed out to me, I perceived we had passed
the dangers laid down in the Charts, which I was in the
act of examining with him on the Quarter Deck when at
three quarters past seven, we felt the Ship take the
Ground abaft, but so very easily that many people on
board were not sensible she had touched. I instantly
made the Signal for the Convoy to avoid the danger and
before they could answer it, we had swung off and with
every hope of not being materially injured, but her
frame was, unfortunately, too slight to sustain any
Shocks whatever. The lower part of her Stern Port had
given way, and her after wooden ends started which occasioned a leak of such magnitude, that all the Pumps
could not keep under. I then made the Signal for the
Convoy to bring to, and send all their Carpenters which
was instantly complied with, but all their exertions combined with those of our own Carpenter and his Crew
were of no avail in reducing the leak altho' every thing
they suggested as likely to be of use, was executed with
the utmost alacrity. We unhung the rudder from the
broken part of the Stern Post, cleared the Bread Room
and Store Rooms abaft—run the Guns and every thing
heavy forward to relieve her from the pressure of their
weight aft—then threw them all over board, Anchors,
etc. to lighten the Ship generally, thrummed a Sail with
Oakum and Tar, and drew it under her bottom and for a
time I was flattered with a hope of getting her into
Trincomalee, but, by four in the Afternoon, notwith-
standing the indefatigable exertions of every Officer and
Man on board, the Water had gained so much as to be
two feet above the Orlop Decks, when the Carpenters
reported that the Ship could not swim much longer; it
then became my duty to preserve the valuable lives of
the Crew, and the painful order for abandoning His
Majesty's Ship was given when the Boys, (unreadable

word) and two divisions of the Seamen and Marines (the others being kept at the Pumps) were put into East India Ships Boats and our own, and to their great credit, with as much order and regularity as if moving from one Ship to another in any of the King's Ports, and when the Boats return'd the remaining divisions and Officers quitted the Pumps and took with them the Hammocks and Cloathes of the whole Ships Company, and when I had ascertain'd that every soul was removed from the Ship I quitted her, with feelings, however painful, that were well supported by a sense of having done my duty, and five minutes afterwards her Mastheads were below the surface of the Water.

I am a collector of coincidences, and as we sailed past the grave of the *Daedalus* on July 7, 1963 I realized that it was 150 years later, *to the very day*, since her unfortunate captain had composed that letter, doubtless chewing anxiously at his quill pen. At the court-martial the next month, he amplified his statement and gave a vivid account of the way in which, even in perfect weather, the Basses contrived to claim a victim:

Proceedings of the Court

At which Captain Murray Maxwell read his own written narrative—which was more detailed than his Letter:

"The Master proposed altering course to the North, which the Captain ordered to be done 'after particularly enquiring if our distance by the Log gave us past the Basses, and being assured by the Master it did so, and some leagues more. . . . but as the directory states, measured distance off that part of the Coast cannot be depended upon. . . .' he was on deck 'looking carefully around with My Glass, and making the Officer of the

Watch and people at the Mast Head to do the same; the Atmosphere being then so perfectly clear that it seemed impossible for any Breaks, or even ripple upon the Water to exist within the limits of our Visual Horizon, undistinguished; and. . . . nothing indicating danger was discovered until the Ship struck, and soon after she came off, the Sun being obscured by a passing Cloud, we plainly perceived the Little Basses, which its strong refracted rays, chancing to fall immediately upon, had prevented our discovering, altho' we had passed inside of, and close to them; and as a further corroboration of this. . . . the *Atlas* four or five Miles astern, and a little to the Eastward of us, actually struck upon the Basses before she perceived them, and from the same cause that prevented our observing them in passing; I afterwards distinctly saw them at a distance of three Leagues, and whenever they may be again Surveyed, I will continue to Assert they will be found to lay considerably farther off Shore than at present laid down in any Chart I have seen; and the Shoal the Daedalus struck upon, about four or five Miles N by W of the Little Basses will, I am convinced be found to lay 7 or 8 Miles from the Land. . . . Captain Maxwell praised the Master, in whom he had the greatest confidence, and said that the Ship touching bottom must have been due either to 'a singular error in all our judgements, or a very serious one in the Charts. . . .' and he was confident it would be found to be the latter. . . . But the cause of her foundering must be alone attributed to her extreme weakness—the shock she received on touching the ground would scarcely have injured any other ship. She was built at Venice, and perhaps never intended by the Enemy to go out of that Narrow Guelph; for when taken into dock at Deptford she was found only to possess the Timbers, and Scantling of an 18 Gun Ship, and tho' found rotten in several places forward, had not been opened Abaft, where she showed great symptoms of debility, by unusual working and straining, whenever it blew fresh, when she also made a considerable Quantity of Water; the weight of the Upper Works and Guns, when she touched crushed her slender Frame to pieces. . . ."

That last sentence well describes what undoubtedly happened to the ship we had been exploring, whether or not her "slender frame" had shown "great symptoms of debility." Perhaps one day we will go in search of the *Daedalus;* but in the hours before she sank she must have drifted several miles from the rock she inadvertently christened, and she probably lies in deep water.

The Court decided, incidentally: That the loss of the *Daedalus* was occasioned by running on a Shoal. . . . owing to their having shaped a course as supposing themselves outside the Basses. . . . and from the glare of light occasioned by the rays of the sun on the water which prevented them seeing the Breakers. . . . and which the Convoy also did not see. It was agreed that every possible means was used by the Captain, Officers and Crew to save the Ship.

Mr. Webster, the Master, was declared guilty of gross neglect of Duty and severely reprimanded. Captain Maxwell was recommended to be more cautious in the future.

In his statement, the Captain praised the conduct of the Officers and men 'with the exception of one Marine who got intoxicated.' He was to be punished, but this was subsequently remitted by Admiral Hood, because of previous good conduct.

Though I feel sorry for the unlucky Captain Maxwell, I cannot help thinking that his account of the disaster is a little contrived. It also contains one major discrepancy that, had the members of the court-martial known of it, might have made them reconsider their verdict.

In his defense, the captain argued that there must be a "singular error in the charts," and added his conviction that the unknown shoal upon which he had struck lay "7 or 8 miles from the land."

Well, it doesn't; the water seven miles out is a safe hundred fathoms deep. Daedalus Rock itself is less than *two* miles from shore.

At the court-martial, someone was stretching the truth— in the ratio of about four to one.

26

Reflections

on Squid

During the night we sailed up the east coast of the island, passing the grave of one ship that has been on our list for several years. Less than a century and a quarter lies between the *Daedalus* and the *Hermes*, yet technologically they are eons apart. For *Daedalus* was a wooden frigate; *Hermes* was the first aircraft carrier. Though earlier ships had been converted to carriers, *Hermes* was the first vessel in any of the world's navies to be designed for this purpose from the keel up. Ordered during World War I, she was completed in 1924, and refitted ten years later. Displacing 11,000 tons, she was almost 600 feet long.

In April 1942 she was in Trincomalee Harbor when news came that a strong Japanese force was approaching, and that an air attack was imminent. On the afternoon of April 8, a Catalina reported a large force four hundred miles east of Ceylon, and—remembering Pearl Harbor—the authorities ordered all shipping out of Trincomalee.

Hermes, the destroyer *Vampire*, the corvette *Hollyhock*, and several merchantmen were sent south and told to hug the coast, but on the morning of April 9 enemy aircraft detected them and attacked in overwhelming strength. *Hermes* went down in twenty minutes; ironically enough, she was not only the first British aircraft carrier—she was the only one to be sunk by aircraft. With her went *Vampire* and *Hollyhock*, and though for some reason best known to the Admiralty the report of the action is still classified as "Restricted," we have been informed that *Hermes* was attacked off Batticaloa in 7°35′ N., 82°5′ E.

The local fishermen claim that when the water is clear they can see the fish clustering round her superstructure about sixty feet below the surface. But here is a slight mystery—the Admiralty position is twenty miles to the southwest of the wreck undoubtedly known to the Batticaloa fishermen. However, *Hermes* could travel this distance in forty minutes, and falling bombs discourage accurate navigation. Perhaps the fisherfolk are right; one day we must investigate. A sunken aircraft carrier would make a unique subject for the underwater camera.

At breakfast time we sailed into the magnificent Trincomalee Harbor, and anchored in the roads next to a large Russian freighter. The port authorities flashed us three messages by signal lamp; the first was, "Are you a warship?" When we had convinced them that we weren't, there was a long pause, then two more messages followed. The second was obviously inspired by a telescopic survey; it wanted to know, "Who are are the girls on deck?" I found this query quite understandable, for there were times on board *Via Vida* when it was easy to believe that we were making screen tests for *Lolita*.

The third message got down to particulars. It asked bluntly "Is Elizabeth Wilson on board?" Mike never succeeded in discovering who sent that one.

After rendezvousing with Hector, who had driven across from Colombo with aqualungs and air compressor (and had been held up at night for half an hour by an angry elephant on the main Colombo-Trincomalee road), we set off up the coast to do some general underwater filming. Our target was Pigeon Island, about ten miles north of Trinco—and the site of yet another British naval calamity.

In August 1795 an invasion force comprising the warships *Diomede, Suffolk, Centurion, Heroine,* with transports and troops, arrived at Trincomalee with a polite note to the Dutch governor, asking him to hand over the keys (which, after some argument, he was sensible enough to do). However, the *Diomede* (an 887 ton, 44-gunner), hit an unknown rock while towing another vessel. She struck with so much violence that, though all her guns were thrown overboard, there was barely time to save the crew before she sank with all stores.

Mike has a fairly good idea of her location and she must be one of the most interesting wrecks in Ceylon waters. Her trail of jettisoned cannon (each weighing several tons), would also be worth following. Unfortunately, when we dived off *Via Vida* we found that the visibility around Diomede Rock was so bad that it was useless to attempt a search.

Fifty miles to the north of Trincomalee, on a shoal known as Mullaittivu, lies another important wreck—and one which may contain the most valuable cargo lying beneath the waters around Ceylon. On November 9, 1885 the 3,462 ton P & O liner *Indus* was steaming south from Madras to Colombo when she went aground at full speed owing to a gross error in navigation. (She was twenty miles off course, and her captain was lucky to get away with a twelve-month suspension of his ticket.)

At high tide, the *Indus* was worked off the shoal, and then had her second piece of bad luck. She came to rest immediately above one of her own anchors, and as she rose and fell in the waves she quickly knocked a hole in her bottom and sank within a few hours. There was no loss of life, but none of the cargo could be saved.

Aboard the *Indus* was a collection of the finest works of art from the Stupa of Bharut, India (second century B.C.) which had been specially selected by the director of Indian Archaeology, General Cunningham. Today, these statues would be priceless—*if* they are still on Mullaittivu Shoal. But we are not certain of this; we know that salvage operations were later carried out on the *Indus* with a view to recovering the indigo and other valuables aboard her. Would the divers also have bothered to bring up what they probably considered to be a few old statues? We rather doubt it, but until our researchers have settled this important point the *Indus* will remain on our list of possibles, not certainties.

I could continue for pages, listing the dozens of vessels that have come to grief around Ceylon, and whose resting places Mike has located. We have dived on about forty of them, almost every one of which has some special interest, though until we went to the Great Basses we never found— or indeed searched seriously for—anything of value. But I will mention only one more, for it concerns the greatest unsolved mystery of the Indian Ocean, and has haunted my mind for many years.

In May 1874 the schooner *Pearl*, 150 tons, put into Galle for water, sailed past the Great and Little Basses, and headed out into the Indian Ocean on her way to Rangoon. On May 10, well out in the Bay of Bengal, she was becalmed, and was observed from the passing liner *Strathowen* about an hour before sunset. Here is the account of what happened then, as reported by a passenger on the *Strathowen.*

> . . . As we came up with her I lazily examined her with my binocular, and then noticed between us, but nearer her, a long, low, swelling lying on the sea, which from its colour and shape I took to be a bank of seaweed. As I watched, the mass, hitherto at rest on the quiet sea, was set in motion. It struck the schooner, which visibly

reeled, and then righted. Immediately afterwards the masts swayed sideways, and with my glass I could clearly discern the enormous mass and the hull of the schooner coalescing—I can think of no other term. Judging from their exclamations, the other gazers must have witnessed the same appearance. Almost immediately after the collision and coalescence, the schooner's masts swayed towards us, lower and lower; the vessel was on her beam-ends, lay there a few seconds, and disappeared, the masts righting as she sank, and the main exhibiting a reversed ensign struggling towards its peak. A cry of horror rose from the lookers-on, and, as if by instinct, our ship's head was at once turned towards the scene, which was now marked by the forms of those battling for life—the sole survivors of the pretty little schooner which only 20 minutes before floated bravely on the smooth sea.

Five of the survivors, including her master James Floyd, were picked up by the *Strathowen*. When he had recovered, Captain Floyd wrote the following report on the sinking of his ship:

On the 10th of May, about 5 P.M.,—eight bells I know had gone—we sighted a two-masted screw on our port quarter, about five or six miles off; very soon after, as we lay motionless, a great mass rose slowly out of the sea about half a mile off on our larboard side, and remained spread out, as it were, and stationary; it looked like the back of a huge whale, but it sloped less, and was of a brownish colour; even at that distance it seemed much longer than our craft, and it seemed to be basking in the sun. . . . I went into the cabin for my rifle, and as I was preparing to fire, Bill Darling, a Newfoundlander, came on deck, and, looking at the monster, exclaimed, putting up his hand, "Have a care, master; that 'ere is a squid, and will capsize us if you hurt him." Smiling at the idea,

I let fly and hit him, and with that he shook; there was a great ripple all round him, and he began to move. "Out with all your axes and knives," shouted Bill, "and cut at any part of him that comes aboard; look alive, and Lord help us!" Not aware of the danger, and never having seen or heard of such a monster, I gave no orders, and it was no use touching the helm or ropes to get out of the way. By this time three of the crew, Bill included, had found axes, and one a rusty cutlass, and all were looking over the ship's side at the advancing monster. We could now see a huge oblong mass moving by jerks just under the surface of the water, and an enormous train following; the oblong body was at least half the size of our vessel in length and just as thick; the wake or train might have been 100 feet long. In the time that I have taken to write this the brute struck us, and the ship quivered under the thud; in another moment, monstrous arms like trees seized the vessel and she heeled over; in another second the monster was aboard, squeezed in between the two masts, Bill screaming "Slash for your lives"; but all our slashing was of no avail, for the brute, holding on by his arms, slipped his vast body overboard, and pulled the vessel down with him on her beam-ends; we were thrown into the water at once, and just as I went over I caught sight of one of the crew, either Bill or Tom Fielding, squashed up between the masts and one of those awful arms; for a few seconds our ship lay on her beam-ends, then filled and went down.

If you think this is an improbable story, I do not blame you; I would not take it very seriously myself, if it had appeared anywhere except in the shipping column of the London *Times*—a paper not noted for sensational journalism. I have the photostat in front of me at the moment (issue of July 4, 1874): it runs to nine column inches of type. For the full story, and a discussion of its authenticity, I refer you to Frank Lane's excellent book, *The Kingdom of the Octopus*.

Ever since I was a boy, I have been fascinated by the giant squid—and I know exactly what triggered my interest. It was the illustration, in Frank Bullen's classic *The Cruise of the Cachalot*, of a fight between a sperm whale and a squid—which must have taken place, incidentally, within a few months of the *Pearl* report.

It was not until many years later that I came upon a third account of such a sighting, in the greatest work of literature that the United States has yet produced:

But one transparent blue morning, when a stillness almost preternatural spread over the sea . . . a strange spectre was seen by Daggoo from the main-mast-head.

In the distance, a great white mass lazily rose, and rising higher and higher, and disentangling itself from the azure, at last gleamed before our prow like a snow-slide, new slid from the hills. Thus glistening for a moment, as slowly it subsided, and sank. . . .

. . . Almost forgetting for a moment all thoughts of Moby Dick, we now gazed at the most wondrous phenomenon which the secret seas have hitherto revealed to mankind. A vast pulpy mass, furlongs in length and breadth, of a glancing cream-colour, lay floating on the water, innumerable long arms radiating from its centre, and curling and twisting like a nest of anacondas, as if blindly to catch at any hapless object within reach. No perceptible face or front did it have, no conceivable token of either sensation or instinct; but undulated there on the billows, an unearthly, formless, chance-like apparition of life. . . .

As with a low sucking sound it slowly disappeared again, Starbuck still gazing at the agitated waters where it had sunk, with a wild voice exclaimed—"Almost rather

had I seen Moby Dick and fought him, than to have
seen thee, thou white ghost!"
"What was it, sir?" said Flask.
"The great live squid. . . ."

The great live squid. Melville's account, penned a quarter
of a century before the story in the London *Times,* has an
unmistakable air of authenticity. (Though that "furlongs"
must be a slip for "fathoms"—a furlong is an eighth of a mile!)
Moreover, there is a striking resemblance between the
weather conditions in the two cases, and the general behavior of the squid as it basked on the surface. And finally,
the *Pearl,* the *Cachalot* and the *Pequod* were all in the Indian
Ocean—just as we were now, aboard *Via Vida.*

The night that we anchored off Pigeon Island, the crew
of *Via Vida* hung a powerful electric lamp over the side, and
started netting the scores of squid that came swarming
around it, darting through the water like torpedos. When I
handled one, I was most impressed by its beauty, and in particular by the lovely blue glow of the luminescent photo-
phores ringing its eyes.

It seemed such a pretty, harmless little creature—its rub-
bery body only six inches long. But then I remembered the
Pearl, just 170 miles due east of us, and the *Cachalot,* 600
miles east of *her* (all three of us, oddly enough, on almost
the same parallel of latitude)—and the *Pequod* perhaps a
thousand miles to our south. I looked at the shadows flitting
through the darkness around the bright circle of *Via Vida's*
light; and presently I decided to go down to my cabin, and
to secure the porthole lest any "monstrous arms like trees"
come crawling hopefully aboard during the night.

27

Prospects
and Retrospects

O
ur cruise on *Via Vida* was more than an unexpected and unplanned (indeed, unplannable) sequel to the Great Basses expedition. Besides taking us to several possible future sites, it made us realize that there are some things that simply cannot be done on a shoestring. We had almost failed because Mike had tried to be skipper, engineer, chief diver, film director, and cameraman. He nearly got away with it, but there was no margin for errors or breakdowns. *Next* time, we would have a large, reliable ship and a large, reliable crew. And there will, I think, be no difficulty in getting both.

Though Artie and Vida tried to persuade us to come to the Seychelles, Madagascar and points west, flagging a lift back to Ceylon from wherever in Africa we chanced to make landfall, we had to turn down their kind offer. Mike was about to start production of his new movie, *Getawarayo*, which as far as I can gather, is a sort of "Wild-Ones-on-Water," with a climax out of *Ben Hur*, but involving hydroplanes instead of chariots. I suspect that he will film the race before he completes the script so that he will know which actors survive.

And for my part, I could not go galloping off into coelocanth territory until I had written this book, already a year overdue thanks to my encounter with that Colombo doorway. Now that it is finished, I am well aware that it is only an interim report, and raises many questions which, perhaps, will never be answered.

The great unknown is still the identity—even the nationality—of the silver wreck. Almost certainly that can be discovered by a detailed, leisurely, and careful examination of the site by a team of properly equipped and trained divers, preferably led by Peter Throckmorton. And it may be found on dry land by one of our researchers, though that depends on time and luck. Clay Blair's *Diving for Treasure* provides a fine example of the way in which, despite misleading clues, the complete bill of lading of a ship can be run to earth more than two centuries after she has sunk. Somewhere, surely, there must still be a record of a ship important enough to carry at least twenty-two guns and many hundredweight of silver, but as yet we have not found it. Perhaps the publication of this book will help to unearth the final, vital clue.

The clues we already have point in different directions. The bronze cannon is undoubtedly English; the little swivel guns, and the patterns on the pistol butts, suggest Oriental workmanship to some experts. The wood samples which Peter Throckmorton sent to the United States Department of Agriculture's Forest Products Laboratory seem to be both of Asian and European origin (See Appendix B). Of course, a European ship in Eastern waters would carry many boxes and wooden objects of local workmanship.

As an example of the way in which the past can swallow up the facts of everyday life, there is the matter of the soda water bottles from the wreck on the landward side of the reef. Here we have a name and a country, clearly stamped on each bottle—Clarke-Romer & Co., Ceylon. A firm that had the equipment necessary for bottling soda water, and was a registered company, should have left *some* record of its existence after a mere hundred years. But though we searched many contemporary papers and books, and inserted an appeal in the local press, we have discovered only two passing references to Clarke-Romer & Co.

One was found by Lyn de Fonseka, the erudite librarian of the Colombo Museum; in the Colombo *Examiner* for October 7, 1846, he came across an advertisement for a "Cholera Preventive or Sedative Mixture" prepared by Clarke & Romer, of Colombo and Kandy. And a gentleman in the Government Information Department telephoned to say that a book published in 1852—*Prodronus Faunae Zeylanicae* by one Dr. Kelaart—lists them among the establishments at which eager readers may obtain additional copies. Perhaps their flair for best-selling titles explains Clarke-Romer's disappearance from the local commercial scene—though their activities were certainly widespread, to have ranged from cholera preventives through soda water to the animal life of Ceylon.

Doubtless we will discover more about Clarke-Romer, eventually, but we have already found enough to confirm our suspicion that the fine wreck on the northern side of the reef is dated around 1850. It will be interesting to visit it again— *when* we have finished with the silver mine a few score yards away.

As for the three hundredweight of silver whose recovery cost us so much sweat, but luckily no blood, it is still sitting in my office while the Archaeological Department and the attorney-general talk the matter over. Meanwhile, we are preparing a comprehensive exhibit of all the main finds, with photographic coverage, for the Colombo Museum; it is my pious hope that it will be open to the public by the time that this book appears. However, it is a well-known fact that museums, quite rightly, refuse to hurry.

Most of the coins we recovered are still locked up in the big twenty-nine to thirty pound masses, and we can be fairly sure that all except those in the outermost layer are in perfect condition. All told, these lumps contain the better part of ten thousand rupees, but we also have hundreds of loose rupees in ones, twos, or small conglomerations of up to a dozen, cemented together with coral and sand. (See Figs. 48 and 59.) Beneath their protective coating, many of these coins are also very well preserved, and after our 1961 expedition we did a crude but effective job of cleaning with battery acid, metal polisher, and elbow grease on some of them.

This time we wished to be more scientific, so when Peter returned to Greece he took a few of the loose coins with him and handed them over to a chemist friend, Dick Russell. I would like to quote from a report that Dick sent us on June 3, 1963:

A microscopic examination of the incrustation revealed sand particles cemented together with calcium carbonate. The sand was made up of particles of quartz, rose quartz, garnet, and a few which looked for all the world like rubies. All of these particles were water worn. There was one curious find—very small sharp bits of obsidian in some of the lumps. The concoidal fractures and razor sharp edges were unmistakable. They were not water worn and they were not abundant. I have visions of a thin blanket of obsidian being laid down when Krakatoa exploded in 1883. A look at some core samples would be interesting. The sand particles make up about 32% (by weight) of the incrustation. The lumps were stained with hydrated iron oxide and the exposed silver was invariably black with a coating of silver sulfide of varying thickness.

This single paragraph raises two separate, and equally fascinating, speculations. I suspect that the particles that "look for all the world like rubies" are, in fact—rubies. The beaches around Kirinda are full of ruby sand, and the great gem-producing region of Ratnapura is only a hundred miles to the north. Ceylon was the locale of Sinbad's fabulous Valley of Jewels, and though the reality is a little less spectacular than the myth, the treasures that must still lie buried in the interior of the island are beyond computation.

The reference to Krakatoa is equally interesting. When this small volcanic island off Indonesia erupted on August 27, 1883, the explosion was clearly heard in Ceylon, two thousand miles away. One correspondent wrote to the *Times of Ceylon* on August 31st, saying that explosions had continued throughout the morning of the 27th and were "of greater magnitude than any ordinary blasting." No other sound in history has ever been heard at such a distance from its source.

The tidal wave reached Ceylon the same afternoon; in Galle Harbor one Captain Bligh (!) observed a fall and rise of eight feet. It is interesting to think that, for a few minutes on the afternoon of August 27, 1883, much of the Great Basses Reef may have been momentarily exposed to the light of day, and its hidden secrets revealed to any watchers on the new lighthouse. Fortunately, by the time it reached Ceylon, the wave had spent most of its strength; in Sunda Strait it was fifty feet high, and took 36,000 lives.

Pumice started drifting into Ceylon a few weeks later; some years ago I met an old man who remembered seeing the *tsunami* ("tidal wave") in Galle, and the porous stones floating on the water. The dust of the explosion went around the world, and what we would now call the fall-out descended upon all countries, after reaching a height of more than seventeen miles.

Dick Russell devised two methods of cleaning the coins, one electrolytic and the other involving a two-bath process. The problem was to dissolve the incrustation without the resulting free sulphur attacking the silver. The first solution was made by dissolving 5 grams of sodium sulphite in 75 cc of water and adding 25 cc of concentrated hydrochloric acid.

After the coral (calcium carbonate) incrustation had been dissolved, the coins were left with a thin but harmless layer of silver sulphide, which was removed with a brightener solution made by dissolving 50 grams of thiourea in 500 cc of water, adding 15 cc of concentrated hydrochloric acid, and bringing the volume up to 1000 cc with water.

For a while, the house stank of hydrogen sulphide as rupees bubbled briskly in Dick Russell's witches' brews, and we cleaned up a few dozen of the coins for exhibition and photography. But most of the small conglomerations were left exactly as they were, with an eye on a possible future souvenir market. There are plenty of single Mogul rupees around, and they are worth only about a dollar each. These coral-encrusted lumps, still smelling of the sea, are far more interesting and romantic than the individual coins that they contain. We would actually be reducing their value if we took the trouble to break them up and clean them.

Some of the large masses of corrosion products, cannon balls, bits of wood, and coral-cemented stone we shipped to Dick Russell and Mendel Peterson for analysis, and one day they will doubtless be the subject of learned papers in the professional journals. Meanwhile Peter Throckmorton's preliminary report on the main 1963 finds will be found in Appendix A; it will probably be modified and extended in due course, but it gives a very good general picture of the material he and Mike hacked out of the seabed. It also gives some faint idea of the amount that must still be there, awaiting a large-scale expedition with plenty of time and good equipment.

Most people, however, will be more interested in the wreck's still untouched riches than its archaeology. They will wonder if, beneath all the silver that undoubtedly remains, there may be gold. Needless to say, we have wondered too; and I hope that some day we shall know.

Of one fact I feel reasonably certain; that this is the first book ever published giving the exact location of a scarcely touched treasure ship, with full instructions on how to reach it. Some readers may wonder, a little sceptically, at such generosity.

Thanks to the southwest monsoon, the reef's most effective guardian, I am not really giving much away. When this book appears, another season will have come and gone; if, with such a start, we cannot keep ahead of any opposition, we do not deserve to do so.

Moreover, we are taking steps—not all of which I propose to mention here—to safeguard the wreck and to obtain official protection for the site; one of the most important means of insuring this occurred during our last expedition. Until 1963, the Great Basses lighthouse could communicate with the land only at night, by flashing lamp; now, it is fitted with short-wave radio. Unauthorized divers around the reef may expect a swift reconnaissance from the small but efficient Royal Ceylon Air Force—or a raid by Mike and his friends in a fleet of 60 m.p.h. hydroplanes.

Whatever the future of this wreck may be, I regard it with equanimity, and a certain detachment. It has given me a series of experiences which very few living men can share, and which are perhaps unique in this generation; nothing can take that away.

Appendix A

I. GENERAL DESCRIPTION OF THE SITE

by
PETER THROCKMORTON

The wreck site is on the south side of the Great Basses Reef, which runs roughly east and west. It is seven miles off shore. Little of the reef is visible above water, although it breaks heavily in any kind of weather. The reef itself is an extension of the sandstone rocks and similar sandstone juts into the sea at Kirinda, where the lighthouse station is located. The reef is affected by both the northeast and southwest monsoons, which blow hard for at least ten months a year, often more.

The sandstone of the Great Basses Rock is heavily overgrown with coral. The wreck lies just beyond the long ridge of the regular coral which forms the first break of the reef. This ridge rises steeply from a coral and rock bottom which slopes gradually out to the beginning of the sandy bottom forty to fifty feet deep, several hundred feet off the rock.

Individual rocks in this ridge of broken coral rise to within eight or ten feet of the surface, and it is upon one of these that the ship apparently struck. From the lie of the cannon and the fact that the four anchors were found together, it seems logical to assume that the ship, standing north toward the land, struck on the outer ridge of coral, bilged herself, and sank just inside the outer ridge of coral. It lies between this outer ridge and the main spine of the reef, which rises to within two or three feet of the surface and on which waves break all year round.

The valley between the two ridges, where the ship lies, is twenty-five to thirty-five feet deep to the bottom, and roughly twenty-five feet to forty feet wide in the wreck area. In most places its sides are steep. Its bottom is filled with sand and small stones broken by areas of grown-up coral, beach rock, and possibly sandstone overgrown with coral.

It seems clear from the lie of the cannons and anchors that the gully in which the wreck lies has contained most of the material which is still preserved, and that the material still lies more or less where it fell after the ship went on the reef, in spite of the tremendous surge set up by waves breaking on the inner reef and, one presumes, on the outer reef during the monsoon. The surge runs at right angles to the direction of the waves.

The distance from the eastern end of the shank of the outermost anchor to the farthest extension of material found in Group E is approximately 150 feet. I believe it can be reasonably assumed that this represents the approximate length of the ship.

Material on the bottom can be divided into five groups:

Group A

Four anchors and four cannon. This can be presumed to be what remains of the ship's bow. There are various ways of interpreting the lie of the anchors, but the most logical one seems to be that anchors 1 and 2 were catted when the ship struck, and that the others were lashed down on the foc'sle head. This cannot be proved, because they could certainly have been turned in different directions as the ship broke up. (All of these anchors are very heavily sea-grown and very badly corroded.) The broken anchor 4 was likely so heavily corroded that it broke under the weight of anchors 2 and 3 pressing down upon it.

Four cannon, each eight feet long, are associated with the anchors, three of them with the cascabels facing east, one with cascabel facing west. The bottom underneath the anchors is sand at the bottom of cracks in the coral. The entire area is very heavily overgrown with coral. There are certainly some small objects in the sand. A much battered and worn unidentified bronze object was recovered from the sand under anchor 1.

Group B

Three cannon, all very heavily overgrown. Their cascabels seem to be pointing west. The area between A and B is an open area of rock bottom without clefts or gullies, although full of sand on the north side. There appears to be little material in this area except for the cannon.

Group C

Thirteen cannon 8 feet long, plus a larger cannon 10½ feet long.

Group D

The shallow water on top of the second reef to the north of the wreck where the two small cannons were found in

1961. This is where one would expect to find many objects from the ship, because of the prevailing direction of the waves, which would tend to sweep light material, which was high up in the ship, over the reef.

GROUP E

This is apparently what is left of the after end of the ship. It is an area approximately 20 feet long by 10 feet wide. The bottom is sand at the eastern end; from there a ridge of rock extends 20 feet to the western end of the wreck area. The entire area is full of material from the ship. It appears that the formation of the reef is such that after the ship sank, most of the material in the after end and lighter material from other parts of the ship was caught in clefts of the rock, and then concreted over. It is possible that the entire area of the bottom of the gully in this area consists of a compacted mass of ballast stone, decomposed iron, silver coins and bags containing them, and small objects from the ship. All the material raised came from this area. The lumps, some of them as much as two feet long by a foot thick, showed clearly that everything was tumbled helter skelter together when the ship sank.

The ship was iron-fastened. When lumps of the ship were broken up, it was possible to measure the holes which marked places where iron fastenings had corroded away. There were many ship nails two centimeters square. I presume that these nails were the ship's fastenings. Other nails, round, were four centimeters in diameter. Mixed with the blackish mass of iron corrosion products in some of the lumps were pitch and/or tar (which gave off a strong odor as the lumps were broken up), and what appeared to be quantities of gunpowder.

It seems clear that the good preservation of the silver is due to the coins being closely associated with corroding iron. The coins which were in actual contact with iron or in a mass of black material, which appeared to be almost pure iron corrosion product mixed with gunpowder and pitch and approximately 20 per cent sand, were almost always in perfect condition. Silver coins were less perfectly preserved when the sand in the lumps was over 80 per cent.

Several different kinds of teak board fragments were found concreted into the lumps, all of them unfortunately impossible to measure, although it is possible to say that some of them were fragments of money boxes and light boxes, and others were part of planks perhaps five centimeters thick.

In the light of my previous experience with shipwrecks, several things struck me about the lie of the material in this wreck and its preservation. I have naturally discussed the problems of preservation of ancient wrecks with other divers, and the subject has been discussed by several writers, notably Frederic Dumas in *Deep Water Archaeology,* and Honor Frost in *Under the Mediterranean.* The general conclusion is that a very large percentage of the damage done to a wreck occurs within a hundred years after sinking, and probably less.

I was especially struck by the similarity in terms of preservation and lie of material in this wreck to the Cape Gelidonya wreck, which is nearly three thousand years earlier, but in deeper water and less affected by wave action. At Gelidonya, elements of copper and bronze had leached out to combine with sand, which was grown over and welded together by marine organisms to form a solid mass. This was identical to the process which seems to have gone on in the Basses wreck.

I have recently discussed this problem with an archeological chemist, Mr. Richard Russell, who says that, speaking in rule of thumb terms, the reaction rate increases 100 per cent for every ten degrees increase in Centigrade temperature. As the water temperature at the Gelidonya wreck averaged 15 degrees at 90 feet, and the average temperature on the Basses Reef must approximate 30 degrees Centigrade, it is apparent that the rate of disintegration in a site like the Basses wreck might reasonably be expected to be one-and-a-half to two-and-a-half times faster than in the deeper site in the Aegean. The action of the surf on the Basses wreck site should also result in a large increase in the amount of oxygen in the sea water, which accounts for the very heavy corrosion of the anchors and cannon. Iron objects in Area E were very heavily corroded; for example the barrel and lock of the pistol stock described below had disappeared almost completely, although the wood was in good condition. One of the pair of pistol stocks raised was completely untouched by teredos, as were many other wood fragments found in the lumps at Area E. This would seem to indicate that the wreck, although smashed almost immediately, probably within a day or two of the time she went on the reef, was broken up in such a way that material from the after end of the ship washed into one area, probably within a year, and the whole mass of material was stabilized in the first few years after the wreck. The material, now stabilized on the wreck site, will probably remain in good condition almost indefinitely, except for the gradual corrosion of the iron, which is now much diminished because the whole mass is covered by sea growth mixed with corrosion products.

DRAWINGS

Although many measurements were taken and an overlay photograph was taken, it was not possible to make an accurate tape triangulation of the site, due to lack of time, the heavy surge which made even working on the bottom extremely difficult, and lack of personnel. However, I am convinced that a tape triangulation would be extremely useful as a means to understanding the site. Also it seems likely that a very good estimate of how the ship broke up could be made if a section of Area E could be made.

CONCLUSIONS

Evidently the wreck of a large ship—length overall not less than 125 feet, possibly longer. No references to Dutch fluyt ships are available to me here, but it is a remarkable coincidence that Landstrom in *The Ship*, p. 155, illustrates a fluyt with twenty-four guns. The fact that all the cannon except the "Long gun" seem to be the same size seems to preclude the cannon having been ballast in a smaller ship. It is equally apparent that a great deal of the material has remained approximately in place, although the wood of the ship has disappeared completely. This is remarkable in view of the nature of the site. Although the wreck providentially was swept into a valley where it had some protection, since the valley was only slightly larger than the hull, the wreck area is directly under the surf during the monsoon and it is hard to imagine a worse situation for preservation of a wreck. In spite of this, much material has stayed in place, and a careful excavation of the site and drawings made to a reasonable standard of accuracy (maximum error five to ten per cent) would probably make some reconstruction of the ship's structure possible.

II. OBJECTS RECOVERED FROM SILVER WRECK

None of the objects found appear to be in proper archaeoligical context, although their general position corresponded to the approximate location where the objects were placed in the ship. Everything had been scrambled into a sort of an omelette of heavier material in the aft end of the ship, which was swept into crevices in the rock in a jumbled mass, filled in with sand, and then covered over with a coat of coralline sea growth. Almost all of the objects recovered are from a two meter square area in the aft end of the ship.

1. Complete pistol stock of very close-grained hard wood. Butt of an identical pistol. Both have bronze caps on butts, chased with a flower pattern of six leaves and six petals, radiating from the central hole which once contained the iron nail or screw which attached the butt plate to the wooden stock. One of the butt plates is damaged. The un-damaged butt plate measures 57 millimeters by 46, and is approximately two- and one-half millimeters thick. One of the pistols has only a butt portion, the grip remaining intact. The other pistol stock is intact although the iron has almost completely disappeared except for fragments of the barrel, which are approximately five millimeters thick, 4 centimeters from the extreme end of the breech. The intact pistol stock is 48 centimeters long. Attached to it is a wooden ramrod capped with an undecorated bronze plate. It has a bronze ferrule five centimeters from the extreme muzzle end of the stock. Bronze ferrule is 27 millimeters long, decorated with a central ridge and 5 smaller ridges at each side. The barrel of the pistol measured 4 centimeters in length and was attached to a raised ridge in the pistol stock by a single iron screw. The trigger mechanism of the pistol has rusted away almost completely. Its strap appears to have extended 10 centimeters towards the butt from the 12 millimeter diameter hole through which the trigger extended, and towards the front end of the pistol three centimeters. Two holes for iron screws are visible, one in front and one immediately behind the trigger hole. The lock mechanism was 13½ centimeters long, measuring from the center of the hole of the screw to which it was attached to its rear end. The rear end of the lock plate is worked into a gradual point. The lock plate was attached by 3 iron bolts. The pistols appear to have been a pair.

2. Fragments of musket or pistol barrels.
    a) Diameter 41 millimeters, length 140 millimeters.
    b) Diameter 31 millimeters, length 125 millimeters.

c) Diameter 39 millimeters, length 80 millimeters.

d) Diameter 27 millimeters, length 80 millimeters.

e) Diameter 32 millimeters, length 60 millimeters.

3. Pistol barrel and balls. Lead balls, some with sprue attached, were found scattered throughout the entire area. The typical pistol ball measures 16 millimeters in diameter; a typical musket ball 18 millimeters.

4. Pestle, bronze, length 23.40 centimeters, with the upper end 3.65 centimeters, the diameter at the lower end 4.45 centimeters. Diameter of central ridge 3.50 centimeters.

5. Grenade with plug intact, still containing gunpowder. Several of these grenades were raised. The metal was in all cases extremely fragile, and it was impossible to avoid breaking them when removing them from the coral. The metal appeared to be crystallized vertically, the "crystals" running at an angle of 90 degrees from the metal of the grenade. They were plugged with hardwood plugs which were tentatively identified as elm or linder (samples of these plugs have been sent to Forest Products Laboratory for identification). In the larger size "shells," the plug was sealed with a coating of tallow. The wall thickness of the grenades averages 12 millimeters.

6. Cannon balls. Many cannon balls were found. A typical one was 7.85 centimeters in diameter. Three others were 8, 10.3, and 8.7 centimeters in diameter. The smaller ones showed a slightly raised "Casting mark" (?) which runs around the "equator" of each ball. The larger cannon balls have no obvious "casting mark."

7. An iron object.

8. The tampon found in the bronze cannon, very hard wood, possibly oak. A hole was bored in its center into which a foxlay hemp string had been inserted as a pullcord. Tampon string was knotted on the inside with a simple overhand knot.

9. Brass or bronze ferrule of pistol described above (1).

10. Tang part of pistol butt described above.

11. Coins, part of wood chest, and coir bag. The wood appears to be teak. It is difficult to determine whether it is part of a wooden chest which held a number of coir bags full of silver, but this seems likely as teak parts of similar thickness were found throughout the area of the silver, as were fragments of coir bags. The whole mass was stuck together with typical corrosion products.

12. Rifle or musket butt plate (?), copper or brass.

13. Shell plug.

14. Cannon tampon.

15. Grenade plug.

16. Pistol butt piece.

17. Pistol butt piece.

18. Grenade plug.

19. Coir bag.

20. Potsherds. White glazed pottery with blue lines. Several kinds of pottery, all very badly broken, were found in the wreck. In addition to the white, very hard fine ware, which resembled bone china or Delft, there were fragments of coarse red brick or terracotta; a coarse reddish clay pot with silvery black lead glaze (fragments only), possibly European domestic pottery, and what appears to be local Indian ware of some kind, part of a pot of rather coarse and badly baked clay, which is red on the outside and black inside.

21. Neck of glass bottle.

22. Earring, apparently copper or brass with gold wash. Green glass beads. Seems to be from northern India, as village women wear the same sort of earring today.

23. Cannon ball and cemented coin.

24. Mold of musket stock, ramrod ferrule.

25. Concreted pottery.

26. Unidentified pewter object.

27. Unidentified iron object.

28. Three pieces black glaze coarse pottery.

29. Fragment of what appears to be canvas bag which was outside the coir bag which contained coins. As these money bags are said to have been sealed upon receipt, it would seem possible that this is evidence that the coins were received from the Surat Mint by the Dutch East India Company in coir bags, and that these bags were then put into canvas sacks which were then sealed. The coir used in the "money sacks" seems identical to the coir used for gunny bags today. The warp consists of two pieces of twisted foxlay, and the woof is threaded in pairs.

30. Copper serving plate, undecorated except for a groove eight millimeters from the rim. Outside diameter, forty centimeters; rim—six centimeters. Has traces of silver plate.

ANCHORS

Four iron anchors. Three of these were in east-west alignment at one end of the gully in which the remains of the wreck lie. Number 4, broken, was at right angles to numbers 2 and 3. Because of the strong wash of breaking and lack of time, it was only possible to measure anchors 1 and 2, but all four appeared to be the same size.

1: shank thirteen feet long
   fluke to fluke twelve feet
   (There may be some inaccuracy in the measurements as the anchors are very heavily overgrown.)

All four anchors have "Splayed" flukes. These were not measured, because any measurement would be inaccurate because of the seagrowth. All the anchors appear to have had a square hold at the end of the shank.

CANNON

It is difficult to determine the exact number of guns in the wreck without having numbered each gun and triangulated each one in place. The guns are very heavily overgrown with coral and very badly corroded, indeed so badly corroded as to form shapeless lumps. It is impossible to determine the position of trunnions without raising and cleaning, not advisable under the circumstances as there are no facilities for preservation, and there is in any case probably very little iron left, due to the nature of the site.

An attempt was made to measure all the cannons. With one exception they were all 8 feet long, allowing for seagrowth. Overall measurement with seagrowth was between 8 and 9 feet. There were 21 of these guns in three groups, where they seem to have fallen as the ship broke up. Cannon Group A contains 4 guns, all undoubtedly 8 feet long. Group B contains 3 guns, also 8 feet long, and Group C has approximately 14 cannon, which are piled more or less in a heap, cascabels in different directions, showing that the cannons tumbled as they fell. The westernmost cannon in Group C is 10½ feet long, allowing for seagrowth.

The bronze gun appears to be a one pounder. Diameter of muzzle 5.1 centimeters. Length overall: 4'7⅛". Marked on the breech: 2 3 23 8. The cannon appears to be very fine casting. All the lines are sharp and well defined. No evidence of corrosion. The touchhole has a hole beside it threaded 20 millimeters deep. This touchhole was found full of gunpowder, when the cannon was cleaned. A sample of the powder has been sent to the Smithsonian institution. The cannon was plugged when found.

SILVER

The silver appears to have been in coir sacks, perhaps packed several sacks to a wood chest. The coir bags held together long enough for the silver coins to have been concreted solidly together, so that when the sacks finally rotted away, the coins remained in the shape of the sacks. The average weight of the sacks or lumps is about thirty pounds. The inside coins are invariably in mint condition.

Appendix B

Letter Identifying Wood from Silver Wreck

UNITED STATES DEPARTMENT OF AGRICULTURE

FOREST SERVICE

Forest Products Laboratory

Madison 5, Wisconsin

Mr. Peter Throckmorton
14 Atlantos Street
Faliron, GREECE

Dear Mr. Throckmorton:

The wood specimens referred to in your letter of May 9 are identified as follows:

1. Tamper or stopper from cannon muzzle (*Teak, Tectona grandis*)
2. Fiber from next to coins (Bamboo)
3. Pistol butt (Walnut, *Juglans regis*)
4. Musket stock (Teak, *Tectona grandis*)
5. Grenade stopper (Teak, *Tectona grandis*)
6. Miscellaneous fragments (Teak, *Tectona grandis*)

7. Box? fragment (Red pine group)
8. Plank? fragment (Lauraceae, possibly the Asiatic genus *Litsea*)

Specimen No. 3, although most commonly referred to as European walnut is also native to the northern teak producing area of Burma. Since it is a part of the pistol the chances are that it is of European origin as you indicated.

Specimen No. 7 I have simply indicated as belonging to the red pine group which includes *Pinus khasya* which also occurs in the teak region as well as the more familiar Scots pine (*Pinus Sylvestris*) of northern Europe. If this were a fragment from a personal chest it would most likely be European. The individual members of the red pine group are not separable anatomically, and hence we cannot be certain as to the exact species represented.

As you had requested, a copy of this letter is being sent to Clarke-Wilson Associates in Colombo, Ceylon, and the grenade stopper is being forwarded to Comdr. Mendel Peterson at the U.S. National Museum.

Sincerely yours,

B. FRANCIS KUKACHKA, in charge
Wood Identification Research
Division of Wood Quality

Appendix C

PRESERVATION OF OBJECTS RECOVERED
FROM THE SEA

The following notes were supplied by Mendel Peterson of the Smithsonian Institution, Washington, on the Preservation of Objects Recovered From The Sea. As many skindivers lose their finds owing to improper treatment after recovery, I feel that this information should be as widely circulated as possible.

PRESERVATION OF WOOD

Wood that has been submerged in water for long periods of time must be thoroughly dehydrated before it can be preserved. This is accomplished by putting it in three successive baths of pure alcohol, each of the baths to last one week. The alcohol, being very hydroscopic, will remove the water. When this has been completed, the wood should be placed in two successive baths of xylene, the first bath requiring one week.

227

When the wood is in the second bath of xylene, paraffin chips should be added until a saturated solution of paraffin is obtained. This will be evident when paraffin becomes re-crystallized around the edges of the solution. The wood should remain in the saturated solution of paraffin for approximately two weeks. At the end of this period, the wood may be removed from the solution and the xylene in the wood allowed to evaporate.

A coat of small crystals of paraffin will be seen on the wood as a result of the process. This excess paraffin on the surface may be removed with a gentle brushing. The specimen then should be perfectly preserved. In effect, this treatment replaces the moisture in the wood with paraffin and permits the wood to retain its original shape.

PRESERVATION OF LARGE IRON OBJECTS

The first step in preserving large iron objects such as gun tubes, solid shot, and wrought iron fittings recovered from sea water is to prepare a bath of five to ten per cent sodium hydroxide. The object should then be cleaned of the cal-careous coating of coral sand and other deposits by gently tapping it with a hammer. After the crust is removed the object should be immediately placed in the bath and allowed to soak for a period lasting four to six weeks. At the end of this period, the bath should be renewed and "mossy" zinc metal should be placed around and on top of the object so that its entire surface is in contact with the zinc. After a day or two the solution will begin to bubble. This indicates that the reaction is going forward. In a few weeks a white deposit will form on the object and the bubbling will stop. This means that the oxygen which was in the surface of the corroded object has left it and has combined with the zinc metal forming the white zinc oxide. The object should be left in the bath for three or four weeks after the above conditions are observed. At the end of this time it should be removed and the white coating dissolved with a mild solution of sulfuric acid. After the object is dried it should be coated with a clear synthetic lacquer or plastic solution to prevent further corrosion. Smaller objects may be coated satisfactorily by dipping them in a solution of hot paraffin. The reaction should be carried out in a heavy iron trough. Any attempt to shorten this routine will probably result in the loss of the object through disintegration.

Objects waiting for the preservative process should be kept under water until they can be put into the chemical bath. An object should never be allowed to dry out even before the crust is removed.

Appendix D

EQUIPMENT USED ON GREAT BASSES
EXPEDITION, 1963

The list that follows will not only be of vicarious interest to many armchair explorers, but may also be of practical value to those fitting out future expeditions. It should be noted, however, that we were never more than ten miles from shopping centers, so were able to purchase most of the necessities of life—a fact which enormously simplified our problems.

Marine Equipment

28-foot cabin cruiser, twin diesel (30 H.P. Coventry Victor engines), fitted with bunks, Calor gas stove, echo sounder, two 50 gallon fuel tanks, anchor chains, ropes, tool-box
Fishing tackle
Charts
Navigation instruments

Diving Gear

2 pr.   Twin aqualung cylinders (140 cu. ft.)
8   Single aqualung cylinders (70 cu. ft.)
6   Aqualung regulators
1   Pressure gauge
8   Face masks
6   Weight belts, 8 pounds
8 pr.   Flippers
6 pr.   Canvas gloves
3 pr.   Overalls
3   Diver's knives
6   Snorkel tubes
2   Spearguns (Alcedo hydraulic)
2   Slates and Crayons
2   Depth gauges
1   Set decompression tables
1   Cornelius Compressor, Type 380
1   Compressor maintenance booklet
1 qt.   Compressor oil
15 gal.   Gasoline
4   Spare plugs
1   Tool box
1   50 ft. Fiberglass measuring tape
6   Surveying rods, weighted
12   Pitons
2   5 pound hammers
1   Crowbar
1   Icepick
1   Ax
1   Shovel
1   Port-A-Lift underwater balloon
1   Auto jack
300 ft.   ½ inch Nylon rope
30   Numbered metal tags

Photographic and Optical Gear

16 mm Movie Cameras

1 Kodak Cine Special, 15, 25, 40, 62, 152 mm lenses
1 Bolex H 16, 12.5 mm wide-angle lens, Bolex underwater housing
1 Beaulieu, 12 mm lens, Ivanoff correcting lens, Rebikoff underwater case, electric drive

Still Cameras

3 Rolleiflexes in Rolleimarine underwater housing, with flash attachment
2 Calypso watertight cameras
1 Topcon, 58 mm lens
1 Exacta, 58, 40 mm lenses
1 Exacta, 105 mm lens
1 Nikon F, 58 mm lens
2 Leicas, 35, 50, 90 mm lenses

20 100-ft. rolls, Kodachrome II
20 Casettes 36-exposure Kodachrome I
20 Rolls Verichrome Pan, 120
10 Rolls Ektachrome, 120
20 Casettes 36-exposure Plus X Pan
50 Flashbulbs, No. 5.
2 Weston Light meters
1 Changing bag
1 Set watchmaker's tools
1 Bicycle pump (for pressurizing camera)
2 Tripods
1 Binoculars
1 Questar Catadioptric Apochromatic Photo-visual telescope, 3½" aperture, 1077 mm. f.l. electric drive, with coupling for Nikon F.

Personal Gear

Sheets, pillows, mats, towels, clothing, toilet gear, etc.
Sun hats
Dark glasses
Suntan oil
Sunburn lotion
Medicine chest
Cooking stove, kerosene fuel
Icebox
Tinned food, drinks—especially chocolate, cocoa, biscuits,
    boiled sweets for divers when working on site.

Miscellaneous

Writing, drawing materials
Battery-powered tape recorder, spare tapes
Battery-powered all-wave radio
Battery-powered loud-hailer
Rubber torches, spare batteries
1 kw, 230 v, 50c/s portable gasoline generator, with cabling
    and set of lights
50 cellophane bags
20 small plastic boxes
6 large biscuit tins (as watertight containers)
Luger pistol, ammunition

Not Available but Desirable for Future Operations

3 walkie-talkies
1 marine radio
1 spare aqualung compressor
1 underwater metal detector (magnetometer type)
3 Hookah diving sets
Raft-mounted air compressor, with airlift, pneumatic drills,
    hammers, etc.
Explosives

About the Author

ARTHUR C. CLARKE was born in Somerset, England. He served in the Royal Air Force in World War II, becoming technical officer in charge of the first experimental Ground-Controlled Approach unit. Working for a time with the American scientists who had developed this equipment, he later assumed command for the RAF. He is a fellow of the Royal Astronomical Society and served as chairman of the British Interplanetary Society for some years.

Mr. Clarke has written a number of books in the field of space. His *Interplanetary Flight,* now in revised edition, was a pioneer in the field of space flight. Other popular titles about space include *The Exploration of Space* and *The Challenge of the Spaceship,* a collection of short pieces on space and its implications for man. He has also written many books for young people as well as science fiction for adults. In *Profiles of the Future* his facile mind plays with things to come in the improbable world we live in.

Some years ago Mr. Clarke developed skill at skin diving. *The Coast of Coral,* about the Great Barrier Reef, resulted from this interest, which also led to the adventure recounted in *The Treasure of the Great Reef.*

Mr. Clarke spends most of his time in Ceylon, with trips to many other parts of the world. In 1962 he went to New Delhi where he was awarded the Kalinga Prize for his general excellence in science writing. In 1963 the Franklin Institute awarded him the Stuart Ballantine Medal for "his soundly-based and prophetic early concept of the application of satellites in the primary human endeavor of communication."

Format by Sidney Feinberg
Set in Linotype Caledonia
Composed, printed and bound by The Haddon Craftsmen, Inc.
HARPER & ROW, PUBLISHERS, INCORPORATED